AMERICAN GULAGS

MARXIST TYRANNY IN HIGHER EDUCATION

AND WHAT TO DO ABOUT IT

OLIVER L. NORTH,
DAVID L. GOETSCH, AND ARCHIE P. JONES

FIDELIS
PUBLISHING

FIDELIS PUBLISHING®
ISBN: 9781956454062
ISBN (eBook): 9781956454079

American Gulags
Marxist Tyranny in Higher Education and What To Do about It

Cover Design by Diana Lawrence
Interior Design by Xcel Graphic
Edited by Amanda Varian

All Scripture is from The Holy Bible, English Standard Version. ESV® Text Edition: 2016. Copyright © 2001 by Crossway Bibles, a publishing ministry of Good News Publishers.

Order at www.faithfultext.com for a significant discount. Email info@fidelispublishing.com to inquire about bulk purchase discounts.

Manufactured in the United States of America

10 9 8 7 6 5 4 3 2 1

Fidelis Publishing, LLC
Sterling, VA • Nashville, TN
fidelispublishing.com

From Oliver L. North

For Betsy,
my magnificent mate, muse, mother of four and
grandmother of eighteen.
Your courage, tenacity, and love have blessed us all.

From David L. Goetsch:

Dedicated with love to my dear family—
Deby, Savannah, Ethan, Matthew, and Henry.
I pray God's blessings on each of you.

From Archie P. Jones

Dedicated to the memory of Daniel Jones,
beloved son, brother, and friend.

CONTENTS

Introduction: Marxist Tyranny in Higher Education—
An Overview   1

Chapter 1: The Damage Begins in
Kindergarten—America's Public
School Dilemma   5

Chapter 2: Agenda of the Left—Discriminating against
Believers and Conservatives While Severing
the Christian Roots of the Academy   13

Chapter 3: Historical Revisionism: Deception,
Division, and Distortion by Marxist
Professors   29

Chapter 4: "Identity Degrees" and the Dumbing
Down of Higher Education   49

Chapter 5: The High Costs of a College Degree
and the Student Loan Debacle   61

Chapter 6: Secular Humanism, Atheism, and
Agnosticism on Campus   73

Chapter 7: The Left's War on God, Country, and
Conservatives   93

Chapter 8: Fighting Back against Marxist Tyranny   109

Epilogue: A Final Word on Marxist Tyranny in
Higher Education   143

Authors' Biographies   149

Notes   153

INTRODUCTION

*Congress shall make no law respecting an establish-
ment of religion, or prohibiting the free exercise
thereof; or abridging the freedom of speech, or of the
press; or the right of the people peaceably to assem-
ble, and to petition the Government for a redress
of grievances.*

— Constitution of the United States–
First Amendment

We begin this book with the First Amendment to the U.S.
Constitution to emphasize the guarantees of freedom of
speech and freedom of religion contained therein. We wrote
this book because these freedoms, along with that traditional
bulwark of the academy—academic freedom—are being
marginalized, suppressed, and even denied with increasing
frequency in colleges and universities dominated by Marxist
professors and administrators.

Institutions once priding themselves on exposing students to a broad range of opinions and teaching them to
think critically about those opinions have morphed into
academic gulags where group think, wokeness, and political
correctness are the norm. In too many American institutions,
Marxist indoctrination has replaced education, historical
revisionism has replaced truth, coerced conformance has

1

replaced independent thinking, and purposeful dumbing down of the curriculum has replaced the pursuit of knowledge. *Tolerance* in these institutions has come to mean unquestioned acceptance of Leftist orthodoxy. In too many universities, the only research allowed is that which supports Leftist thinking.

America's system of colleges and universities was once the best in the world. Few institutions or organizations contributed more to the success of our nation than the academy. Colleges and universities played a major role in making America the most powerful, productive, and prosperous nation on the globe. Research universities helped make America the world's leader in cutting-edge technologies. Institutions of higher education of all types from community colleges to state colleges to major universities have equipped countless young people to be productive, self-sufficient, contributing citizens of a pluralistic nation. For decades, the key to upward mobility in America was completing a college degree.

Although it still performs well in such disciplines as science, technology, engineering, math, medicine, and business, the academy's status as the scholastic envy of the world is being undermined by Marxist professors more interested in tearing down America than preparing students for the real world. As a result, too many students pay too much and get too little from the college experience.

A lot of college students are being cheated out of a real education and made to believe the world they will inhabit after graduation is like the fantasyland college and university campuses have become. They are graduating with degrees equipping them for nothing more than minimum wage jobs they could get with a high school diploma. Then, to add insult to injury, many of these underprepared graduates are buried in student debt they have no hope of ever paying off.

In 2022, President Joe Biden attempted to push through an unconstitutional executive order to have the American taxpayer fund "forgiveness" for student loan debt. This is not a new idea, but one the Democrat Party has targeted for some time as another ploy to get and keep voters.

Beginning in the 1960s, America's colleges and universities—institutions traditionally reflecting the values of American society—were slowly but steadily taken over by Marxist professors and administrators bent on using their positions to advance an agenda blatantly at odds with the purposes of higher education, an agenda running counter to traditional American values.

Institutions once focused on teaching, learning, research, and introducing students to a broad spectrum of ideas—all protected by academic freedom—transformed themselves into academic gulags. In these "camps," students are indoctrinated instead of educated, coddled instead of challenged, force-fed wokeness instead of being taught critical thinking, taught to value political correctness over freedom of speech, subjected to historical revisionism rather than truth, and restricted to hearing the views of Leftist ideologues rather than a broad range of views, including those of Christians and Conservatives.

As a result, college and university campuses have become dangerous places for Christians, Conservatives, and anyone else seeking an education rather than an over-priced, one-sided social experience. *American Gulags: Marxist Tyranny in Higher Education and What You Can Do about It* was written to help taxpayers, churches, parents, and students not just fight back against the tidal wave of Marxism that has enveloped colleges and universities but win the battle.

As a note to our readers, throughout this book, we will refer to "the Left or Leftists" and "Progressives." We use these monikers interchangeably to identify those who prefer

Marxism over our Constitutional Republic—those who want to tear our nation apart so it can be rebuilt to their vision of total government control and the subjugation of its citizens. However, these are the current labels radicals prefer and are likely to change as they have since the words' origins. Among the most devious and destructive strategies of this group has been the perversion of the English language, what we've previously referred to as "semantic subterfuge."

CHAPTER 1

THE DAMAGE BEGINS IN KINDERGARTEN–AMERICA'S PUBLIC SCHOOL DILEMMA

The focus of this book is Marxist tyranny in higher education. However, many American students have been subjected to twelve years of indoctrination in the name of education before they get to college. Worse yet, their parents have no idea what they are being subjected to five days a week nine months a year. Therefore, a brief examination of what takes place in many of America's K-12 government schools is in order at this point.

Now is a good time to point out this perversion of education has not been at the hands of many teachers. This chart shows how the system has become bloated with "administrators" replacing critically needed, hands-on teachers. If you ever wonder how all the money schools get is spent, and why teacher salaries remain low, often having to supplement classroom materials out of their own pockets. Here's a clue:[1]

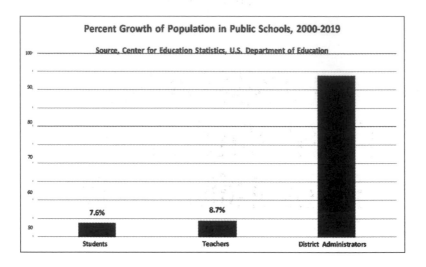

America's educational system is turning young people into compliant, unthinking, ill-equipped minions of the Left who reject the values that made America great, are blatantly ignorant of America's history, view our nation as an evil empire, and think their rights come from government. Many students who attend government schools graduate not having mastered the fundamentals of reading, writing, and arithmetic.

Worse yet, they are happy to have achieved nothing more than functional literacy, if they achieve that. Since we attended public schools, the education system in America has gone from teaching classical literature and calculus in high school to teaching remedial English and math in college. Because of Marxist indoctrination and the dumbing-down phenomenon, many high school students currently graduate unprepared for college, the workplace, or the military.

Not only do these high school graduates not know what they should, they don't even know they don't know, nor do many of them care. Barely literate high school graduates don't realize they have been cheated out of an education by a system more interested in promoting Leftist orthodoxy than intellectual development and character building. Colleges and universities play a major role in the Marxist indoctrination of American students, but the damage begins in kindergarten.

Young people are more pliable than their elders. This makes it easier to mold their character and influence their thinking. This is why Horace Mann, often referred to as the father of American public education, thought children should be placed under the guidance of public school teachers at an early age. Mann thought intellectual and character development were the responsibility of government schools, not parents. Like the Leftist ideologues who control public education today, Mann thought parents were unqualified to take responsibility for the education of their children.

Never mind government schools were originally designed to partner with parents who were responsible for the education and development of their children. Since Mann's time, Leftist Progressive ideologues have taken up his banner and are working hard to remove parents from the equation when it comes to educating America's youth. Like Mann, they believe parental involvement in the education of children should be nil or at the very least limited.

This agenda reached what we can only hope is its zenith as we write this. The pandemic lockdown and school closures in 2020 and 2021 had the unexpected consequence of revealing to parents exactly what was going on behind school doors. Sex education for lower grade elementary kids, including same-sex options, and "transsexual"/drag queen displays was revealed to the horror of many thousands of parents. The major upset election of Glenn Youngkin in Virginia was carried by the exposure of the radicals running government schools and his commitment to put a stop to them.

When it comes to public education, things have changed over the years, to say the least, and not for the better. Although there are still teachers, principals, and school districts rejecting Marxist indoctrination in favor of traditional teaching and learning, their voices are being drowned out by an aggressive majority. Many teachers and administrators who have not bought into the Leftist ideology permeating public education are just holding on hoping to be able to retire and get out of the system. Some who aren't yet close to retirement are going along to get along.

God bless teachers and administrators who are trying to be good stewards of true education. Unfortunately, they represent a minority too small to overcome the Marxist tyranny ubiquitous in government schools. Further, the hard truth is if their predecessors back in the 1960s had stood up to the Marxist ideologues who were beginning to take control of government schools, the onslaught of Leftist ideologues could have been stopped.

The American Left has transformed our public schools from institutions of learning into centers of Marxist indoctrination wherein wokeness is the guiding principle. All too often today's public schools are characterized by the following:

- Dumbed-down curriculums
- Accepting mediocrity and discouraging excellence
- Worship of diversity (except diversity of thought, opinion, and beliefs)
- Demands for tolerance of everything except Christianity, conservatism, and traditional American values
- Portrayal of America as an evil nation
- Distortion of history to fit the false narrative of the Left
- Refusal to give parents a say in what their children are taught
- Advocacy for wokeness including teaching such academic tripe as Critical Race Theory and the 1619 Project

The transformation of public education in America raises three important questions. First, what is the purpose of education? Second, how does indoctrination differ from education? Finally, who is responsible for the education of America's children? Every parent whose children attend public schools should know the answers to these questions.

THE PURPOSE OF EDUCATION

The purpose of K-12 education is to prepare students to be productive, contributing members of a pluralistic society and to equip them to achieve their highest potential. To this end, we have traditionally expected young people to graduate from high school prepared to take care of themselves in a responsible manner while also contributing to the good of their communities and our country. We have traditionally expected high school students to be prepared upon graduating to enter the workplace, college, or the military and succeed.

The purpose of education cannot be fulfilled by dumbing down curriculums, discouraging excellence, disallowing opinions that differ from Leftist orthodoxy, suppressing Christian and conservative thought, rejecting traditional values, engaging in historical revisionism, excluding parents from their children's education, and advocating the false principles of wokeness. A business that fails to fulfill its purpose is soon shut down, yet Americans continue to support colleges and universities that fail to fulfill their purposes.

INDOCTRINATION IS NOT EDUCATION

Indoctrination is not education; it has a much different purpose. While education encourages intellectual development, critical thinking, academic excellence, creativity, and curiosity, indoctrination limits and even discourages these things. Education expands the horizons of students but indoctrination limits them. Education results in growth and development, but indoctrination inhibits both.

Education broadens one's views, but indoctrination limits them. Education encourages debate, informed disagreement, openness to new ideas, and exposure to a wide range of opinions, worldviews, and perspectives. Indoctrination discourages all of these things and, instead, demands intellectual submission, obedience, and conformity. Education is about teaching people how to think and then letting them draw their own conclusions. Indoctrination is about teaching people what to think and discouraging nonconforming conclusions. Education seeks to expand the ability of people to think independently, but indoctrination discourages independent thinking.

PARENTS ARE RESPONSIBLE FOR THE EDUCATION OF THEIR CHILDREN

The Leftist ideologues who control public education believe they, not parents, are responsible for the education of children. They don't accept that parents *hire* teachers through their taxes to assist them in educating their children. They don't understand that acting *in loco parentis* means acting on behalf of parents by helping perform some of the parents' responsibilities. It does not mean taking over the responsibilities of parents. The parents who pay for public education sit at the top of the educational hierarchy, not teachers, principals, or school board members.

Leftist faculty members and administrators don't welcome input from parents because thinking mothers and fathers might have high expectations. In addition, they might ask inconvenient questions Marxist ideologues cannot answer. To fend off parents who might not approve of what they are doing, the Left claims that matters of curriculum, content, and methodology should be left to education professionals.

This is like saying you should leave decisions concerning your children's clothing to the retail professionals at Wal-Mart, and that you should have no say in the matter. What nonsense. Your children belong to you, not the government, just as they don't belong to Wal-Mart. Further, just as you pay for the clothing purchased at Wal-Mart, you pay for public education. Therefore, the public schools are supposed to be servants of the parents and taxpayers who finance them.

THE PROBLEM WITH TEACHERS' UNIONS

Many of the teachers in America's government schools are members of a teachers' union. This wouldn't be a problem if these unions invested their substantial resources in the improvement of educational quality, curriculums, teacher qualifications, and textbooks, but they don't. In fact, if you examine their positions on educational issues, it would be easy to conclude teachers' unions care little about students and steadfastly oppose policies that would improve the quality of education provided by government schools.

Consider some of the perennially high-priority issues of teachers' unions. They include the following: higher pay for teachers irrespective of performance, seniority-based employment practices instead of merit-based practices, opposition to school choice for parents, opposition to vouchers parents can use for private or charter schools, less time in the classroom although their work days and work years are shorter than those of other professions, and opposition to being held accountable for the performance of their students. Not surprisingly, teachers' unions are dependable supporters of the Democratic Party and Leftwing politicians.

A FINAL NOTE TO PARENTS

It is important for parents to understand that the government school they attended years ago is not the government school their children are attending, even if it is housed in the same building and still has the same name. If your school was named after one of the Founders such as George Washington or Thomas Jefferson, chances are its name has been changed to mollify Leftist ideologues as part of the cancel culture. However, even if the name is the same, the curriculum, textbooks, and teaching philosophy may be radically different than those you remember with fondness.

If your children attend government schools controlled by Leftist ideologues bent on turning them into Marxist minions, the best thing you can do is take them out of those schools. You have options. Christian schools, charter schools, and homeschooling are all available to you. Reforming government schools, though a noble cause, will take decades. By the time that battle is eventually won—if it ever is—your children will already be thoroughly indoctrinated. They will, then, be turned out into the real world ill-equipped and underprepared. This fact is what has created the *boomerang phenomenon* in which unemployable adult children move back home after college and live with their parents.

CHAPTER 2

AGENDA OF THE LEFT– DISCRIMINATING AGAINST BELIEVERS AND CONSERVATIVES WHILE SEVERING THE CHRISTIAN ROOTS OF THE ACADEMY

Free speech and free thought are two of the founding principles of our nation. Based on what is happening on college campuses in the twenty-first century, one cannot reflect on this fact without a measure of trepidation. Because free speech and free thought are being regularly and systematically denied on college campuses, we fear for the future of higher education in America and, by extension, the nation. Make no mistake about it, the two futures are inextricably linked.

America's institutions of higher education are perpetrating tyranny by suppressing free thought and free speech. The most frequent targets of this kind of abuse are Christians and Conservatives. By suppressing the free thought and free speech of this substantial segment of America's diverse population, they are undermining the very purpose of higher education.

Even in this age of Marxist tyranny, most colleges and universities still claim to fulfill the following purposes: 1) discovery of new information through research and scholarship, 2) imparting knowledge through teaching and learning, 3) transmission of knowledge to society at large, 4) exposure of students to a wide range of opinions, worldviews, and ideas, 5) helping students become independent, critical thinkers, and 6) equipping students to be productive, contributing members of a pluralistic society.

Universities controlled by Marxist ideologues fall short in achieving all of these purposes. In these institutions, research that questions Leftist orthodoxy is discouraged, articles published in scholarly journals must reinforce the tenets of Leftist orthodoxy, students are not allowed to hear the views of Christian or conservative speakers and few Christian or conservative professors are hired, students are taught what to think instead of how to think and are discouraged from questioning the Marxist party line, and students are channeled into meaningless degrees with no value in the marketplace.

Are all colleges and universities in America controlled by Marxist ideologues? No, they aren't. There are still some dedicated to fulfilling the traditional purposes of higher education instead of advancing a Leftist agenda, but they are in the minority. If you are reading this book and work at or attend a college or university still committed to the fundamental mission of higher education, do not be offended—we are not talking about your institution.

This book was written in response to what is happening at the majority of our nation's flagship universities, those setting the tone and leading the way in higher education. These universities tend to be the larger institutions of higher education in their respective states, although many smaller institutions have followed their lead. These well-known and highly respected universities are now dominated by Marxist faculties actively silencing Christian and conservative students and professors as they seek to consolidate power and advance their Leftist agendas.

FREE SPEECH ZONES–SUPPRESSING FREE SPEECH AND THOUGHT

Marxist institutions use a variety of methods for suppressing speech and thought that does not comport with Leftist orthodoxy. In most cases, this means suppressing Christian and conservative thought and speech. Marxist professors belittle students whose views are at odds with theirs, colleges and universities publish lists of words and phrases banned on campus often labeling them as *hate speech*, review committees deny admission to graduate school to Christians and Conservatives who have been vocal in expressing their views, newly entering freshmen are required to attend *sensitivity seminars* in which they are encouraged to accept what to them may be unacceptable, and students who turn in essays and theses extolling Christian or conservative views are graded down or even failed.

Perhaps the most blatant method for suppressing Christian and conservative speech and thought is the so-called *free speech zone*. A free speech zone is a designated area on campus—often in a remote location—where students are allowed to express their views, provided they have received prior approval of the institution's administration. Setting aside the fact that every square inch of a college or university campus should be a free speech zone, this underhanded method illustrates just how low Marxist ideologues will go in trying to suppress dissenting opinions.

Granted free speech can be loud, disruptive, and even obnoxious; but lest we forget, accommodating free speech is a Constitutional mandate. Our republican form of democracy is, has always been, and will always be messy. Taking appropriate steps to protect teaching, learning, and campus life from disruption is an appropriate undertaking for a university administrator. However, using so-called free speech zones to suppress free speech is not the way to go about it, nor is that why Marxist institutions establish free speech zones.

The trend is to locate free speech zones in isolated areas of the campus as far away from student traffic as possible and to limit certain kinds of speech to tightly restricted times and days. Students who want to exercise their Constitutional right to free speech are typically required to complete an application well in advance, summarize what they plan to say, and even provide personal information. This requirement is blatantly unconstitutional. Another error universities are making is treating non-disruptive activities in the same way they treat disruptive activities. For example, a Christian student talking about Jesus Christ to passersby is hardly the same as students rioting.

OTHER TACTICS FOR SUPPRESSING CHRISTIANS AND CONSERVATIVES

College and university campuses controlled by Marxist professors and administrators have become cloistered enclaves completely out of touch with the real world. Marxist ideologues callously believe they can get away forever with their discriminatory practices against Christians, Conservatives, and anyone else who refuses to toe the line of Leftist orthodoxy. Here are just a few of the tactics the Marxists who control higher education use to carry out their war on students who still subscribe to traditional American values:

• *Making derogatory and belittling remarks.* Publicly humiliating students who refuse to comply with Leftist orthodoxy is a common practice among Marxist professors.

The point of this tactic is to embarrass Christian and conservative students into compliance or, at the very least, silence.

- *Denial of admission to graduate school.* Students who are outspoken in their rejection of Marxism are often denied admission to graduate school and have to file suit to reverse this blatantly unconstitutional situation. The denials are issued in spite of the fact that the Christian and conservative students in question have high scores on the Graduate Record Examination (GRE) and in their lower division courses.

- *Refusal to award degrees.* This is a corollary to the previous tactic used just in case a Christian or conservative student somehow slips through the admission process. The goal is the same: keep the "club" pure by denying access to those who reject Marxism.

- *Denial of promotions.* In spite of the efforts of Marxist ideologues who hire only like-minded professors, a few Christians and Conservatives occasionally slip through. Further, a few professors who begin their careers as Marxists see the light and become educators instead of indoctrinators. Consequently, Marxists must have another tactic for limiting the impact of professors whose leanings are not sufficiently to the Left. One such tactic is to deny them promotions. When Marxist professors control university faculties—which is now the norm—they can also control who is promoted and who is not, irrespective of scholarly merit.

- *Denial of tenure and terminations.* This tactic is aimed at professors who refuse to comply with Marxist expectations. In a major university, denial of tenure is the academic equivalent of the death sentence. Once tenure has been permanently denied, the next step is termination.

- *Demotions.* This tactic is aimed at professors who reject Marxist ideology but have already earned tenure. Once tenured, it is difficult to terminate a professor regardless of his or her political or religious views. However, Marxists still have an effective tactic available to them: demotion. Tenured professors in universities compete tooth and nail to teach the more prestigious graduate courses in their fields. Teaching freshman and sophomore courses is often relegated to graduate teaching assistants. However, when a department controlled by Marxists wishes to punish a faculty member for refusing to toe the Leftist line, demoting that individual to teaching introductory-level courses is an effective and increasingly prevalent tactic.

• *Threats and intimidation.* At times, the feuds within departments of major universities get ugly. Christian and conservative students, professors, and guest lecturers often receive threats and are sometimes victims of various forms of intimidation ranging from petty provocations to more serious actions. For example, it is not uncommon for conservative speakers on university campuses to be shouted down and even pelted with pies, excrement, and bottles. Some have received death threats.

We cover the Left's war on Christians and Conservatives in detail in chapter 7. At this point, suffice it to say there is a war underway on university campuses and the Left is winning.

WHAT EVERY COLLEGE STUDENT SHOULD BE ABLE TO EXPECT

Should Christians and Conservatives have to sell their souls to get a good education in America? Should they have to check their values at the door of a university classroom? Should Christians have to choose between winning on the university campus or losing their faith? We are asked these types of questions all the time, and our answer is always the same: a resounding NO. The freedoms granted to all Americans in the Constitution, including freedom of speech and freedom of religion, are on the side of Christians; even at universities and colleges. However, Christians and Conservatives who wish to exercise these freedoms in today's university environment should be prepared to fight the good fight. Chapter 8 of this book contains recommendations on how to carry the fight for your rights into the lions' den— and win.

Ideally, Christian and conservative college students should be able to expect their views to be heard and received with respect and their right to hold those views acknowledged. Their religious and political views should not negatively impact their studies, college experience, or success in pursuing the degrees of their choice. This expectation will not be realized if Christians and Conservatives simply give up and cede control of universities to the radical Left. If Christians are going to fulfill their God-given dominion mandate, they must first fight to regain it. America's institutions of higher education represent one of the key battlegrounds in this struggle.

On the other hand, an America and, in turn, a higher education system that once again recognizes the sovereignty of God is a goal that could take a good while to achieve. While work is underway to accomplish this goal, there are thousands of Christian and Conservative students who, in the interim, must decide what to do about college. This being the case, these students and their parents can be forgiven for asking: "What about right now? What should we be able to expect—even demand—from universities in the short term?"

Christian and conservative students should be able to attend any institution of higher education in America with full assurance that their values and rights will be respected.

More specifically, they should be able to expect universities to live up to the bedrock values of higher education, values including the pursuit of truth, free inquiry, free speech, free thought, pluralism, respect for diversity, openness, and fairness. They should be able to expect an environment in which the following assumptions are true:

- Faculty members are hired, promoted, and granted tenure on the basis of competence and merit. Further, political and religious views are not factors in the hiring, promotion, or tenure approval processes.
- Students are graded solely on merit, not on the basis of their religious or political views.
- Students are granted admission to graduate studies on the basis of merit, not their religious or political views.
- Students are exposed to a wide range of worldviews, encouraged to think critically about them, and expected to arrive at their own conclusions. Dissenting opinions are welcomed, encouraged, and received with respect.
- The teaching and learning environment is conducive to the civil exchange of ideas so students and professors may disagree without being disagreeable. Academic freedom and intellectual pluralism guaranteed and practiced in ways to ensure the integrity of the teaching and learning environment.
- Differing points of view may be expressed with full assurance they will be given a forum and accorded the respect they deserve.

Colleges and universities that cannot assure students the assumptions just listed are true in practice are not living up to their obligations as institutions of higher education nor are they carrying out the purposes of the academy. All students should be able to rely unequivocally on the reality of these assumptions, and now more than ever.

Today's college graduates enter a world vastly different from the one their predecessors encountered after college. There has never been a time in America's history when cultural uncertainties made life more difficult to navigate. People now demand the right to choose their gender denying their biological sex at birth, transgendered men demand the right to compete against biological women regardless their scientifically-proven physical advantages, life has lost its meaning due in part to the thriving abortion industry, drug abuse and gun violence have reached epidemic proportions, drivers are shot and killed in road rage incidents for simply driving too slowly, teen suicides are at an all-time high, the traditional family has been torn asunder by divorce and same-sex marriages, and the primary means of communication has become "social" media.

No wonder today's college-age generation is confused. It should be. Colleges and universities have no business adding to the confusion by undermining the one worldview that equips people to navigate the moral fog generated by America's cultural identity crisis. Dealing with these confusing cultural issues requires learning to think critically. It also requires developing an understanding of what it means to be human, an understanding only found in Holy Scripture. Attacking, reviling, and suppressing the views of those who turn to the Bible to find answers to complex cultural enigmas is behavior unworthy of colleges and universities claiming to be institutions of higher education.

SEVERING THE CHRISTIAN ROOTS OF HIGHER EDUCATION

The historical record is clear—America was founded on Christian principles. It is ironic, then, that in the colleges and universities of today it is often Christians and Conservatives who are oppressed. Just as America was founded on

Christian principles, so were America's universities; although this fact is unknown to many who are indoctrinated in Left-leaning schools in which *freedom-FROM-religion* is taught as gospel.

America's first colleges were a fundamental part of a Christian society which honored intellectual achievement as an important means of glorifying God, required much of its students, demanded a learned clergy, and was interested in virtually every area of life. Unfortunately, much has changed over the years and not for the better.

That today's college students are ignorant of the Christian heritage of higher education is not surprising. American students are increasingly out of touch with all aspects of our nation's history; a sad situation unto itself but not the most disturbing part of the problem. After all, ignorance is curable. The more significant aspect of the problem is even when they know their history, many students have been conditioned to deny it or be ashamed of it. Rather than being taught to seek the truth, they have been misled by the Marxist education system's anti-Christian, anti-conservative agenda.

In many universities today, to advocate a fair hearing for the truth of the historical record is to bring the wrath of the system crashing down on you. This overt anti-Christian crusade is a fairly recent development. Universities in this country have a long history of being more liberal than the American public at large—there is nothing new in this. However, their propensity for condoning and even encouraging the suppression of Christian and conservative thought is a relatively new development that has emerged gradually since the end of World War II. What is happening on the campuses of many major universities today is downright Orwellian. Through the persistent and effective application of revisionist history, Marxist faculties are denying the past and dominating the present so they can control the future.

To understand how a system of higher education origi-nally built on a foundation of Christian principles could have retreated so far from these principles, one must begin at the beginning. America's oldest and most revered institutions of higher education were all church affiliated in the begin-ning. Consider the following lists of our nation's oldest and most widely-recognized universities. These institutions are known worldwide and revered by many, but without excep-tion they have strayed far from their Christian roots. In order of longevity, America's oldest universities and their religious affiliations are:

- *Harvard University* (1636): Puritan Congregational Affiliation
- *The College of William & Mary* (1693): Anglican Affiliation
- *Yale University* (1701): Congregational Affiliation
- *Princeton University* (1746): Presbyterian Affiliation
- *Columbia University* (1754): Anglican Affiliation
- *Brown University* (1764): Baptist Affiliation
- *Rutgers University* (1766): Dutch Reformed Affiliation
- *Dartmouth College* (1769): Puritan Affiliation

As the religious affiliations of America's first colleges and universities show, the Christian heritage of higher education in this country in indisputable. Unfortunately, it is a heritage that for the most part is now denied by Marxist revision-ists in many of America's major universities. The founders of America's first colleges would neither recognize nor appreci-ate what their institutions have become.

America's earliest colleges reflected the values of the society they served: Christian values. This is as it should be. In order to serve society, universities must be in touch with society. Unfortunately, in a time when the Left dominates so many university campuses this is typically not the case. Today many universities are not just out of touch with the values of American society, they are completely at odds with these values; which, of course, is why they work so hard to undermine them. Universities give a great deal of lip service to tolerance, but in practice they are increasingly intolerant of views lacking the radical Left's seal of approval; views such as Christianity and Conservatism.

Increasingly, Marxist faculty members advocate world-views openly hostile to Christian and conservative values. Many of America's major universities have become self-val-idating, self-perpetuating enclaves of Leftist thinking, iso-lated and insulated from the very society they purport to serve and are supposed to serve. However, because they are seques-tered from American society, many of our colleges and uni-versities serve only themselves. This fact threatens the future of higher education in this country and, in turn, the country because the futures of the two are inextricably linked.

EXPELLING GOD FROM HIGHER EDUCATION

The sinful nature of man is such that America's first institu-tions of higher education wasted little time in beginning their retreat from Christian values. However, as is often the case with such situations, progress toward the secularization of higher education was originally slow and incremental. The *boiling-the-frog syndrome* has always been a favored tac-tic of anti-Christian movements.

The movement to expel God from college picked up steam in America following World War II and really gained traction during the turbulent 1960s. As a result, the radical Left has made great strides toward its goal of dominating university faculties. Without question, the Left understands that in order to control the hearts, minds, and values of future generations, they must first control the faculties of flagship universities; those setting the trends and providing leadership for other institutions of higher education. Even a cursory look at what is happening on the campuses of America's major universities will show how the Left has not only made progress, but is winning the battle. Not only does God no longer have a seat in the classroom, He has been expelled from college.

False Gods on Campus

It is not religion per se but Christianity specifically has been supplanted on the campuses of Marxist institutions. Today's radical Left professors are just as religious as were their academic predecessors who founded higher education in America. The difference is the radical Left worships at the altar of secular humanism rather than the feet of God. Their relativistic religion is not just man-centered, it is "me"-centered. Consequently, the ultimate god of the Left is not just the individual; it is the specific individual who happens to have power, control, or influence in a given situation. This is a convenient worldview if you wish to be the ultimate authority concerning right and wrong—which is precisely what the radical Left in America's universities wants.

Moral relativists reject Christ and the apostles while deifying the ancient Greek and Roman philosophers. Studying Aristotle, Anaximenes, Diogenes, Heraclitus, Plato, Socrates, Xenophon, and the other giants of the ancient Greek and Roman worlds is certainly a worthy undertaking and should be part of the college experience, but elevating them to the level of deity is overdoing it. Christian scholars also study the Greek and Roman philosophers and acknowledge their contributions. But unlike their Marxist colleagues, Christian scholars do not deify them or turn them into saints. Rather, they know Plato, Aristotle, Socrates, and the other giants of the ancient world had feet of clay—as all men do. Moreover, they know the religious and philosophical failures of the views of these ancient man-centered thinkers.

In fact, freedom in the ancient world of the Greeks and Romans—who are so admired by Marxist professors—meant freedom to make the laws. Ancient Greek and Roman leaders understood those who make the laws rule. This is why the radical Left has worked so hard to gain the upper hand in university faculties. If they can dominate academic departments, they can determine who receives tenure and who does not, the content of courses, the books to be used when teaching courses, how controversial and unsettled social, ethical, economic, and political issues are handled, and—most important of all—how the concept of academic freedom is interpreted and applied.

ACADEMIC FREEDOM:
WHAT IT SHOULD BE BUT ISN'T

Academic freedom is a widely misunderstood nebulous concept and increasingly abused by Marxist faculties. As they have with so many concepts—inclusion, tolerance, equality—Leftist ideologues have turned academic freedom on its head.

The first thing we should understand about academic freedom is it is an academic tradition, not a Constitutional guarantee. This means it is defined and enforced by college and university faculties not the law. None the less, if properly interpreted and applied, it can be a useful protector of free thought. However, if misused by a majority determined to maintain control and advance a specific agenda, it can be an effective instrument of suppression. In many cases, this is what it has become.

Academic freedom is intended to ensure students, professors, and other education professionals are allowed to hold and openly express their own views while also exercising their personal judgment in matters of scholarship including teaching, writing, and research. Further, they are to be able to do these things without fear of retribution or other negative consequences. Academic freedom, when properly applied, is important because it encourages a broad range of views and allows the prevailing orthodoxy to be questioned and even challenged.

Colleges and universities should be "safe havens" for discussion and the reasoned debate of diverse ideas. Students and faculty should be allowed and even encouraged to challenge conventional wisdom in any field. This ideal, if actually realized, can strengthen society. Further, putting ideas to the test can, in fact, teach students to think and sharpen their skills at defending their worldviews. This is what is meant in Proverbs 27:17 where we read: "Iron sharpens iron, and one man sharpens another." This statement encapsulates the theory of academic freedom. Unfortunately, it's a theory that often breaks down is in its application.

If scholars should be encouraged to question the prevailing orthodoxy in any field, why are those who challenge the conventions of Marxism demonized, shunned, failed, refused admission to graduate school, denied tenure, and even fired? If universities truly want to teach students how to think and defend their ideas in reasoned debate, why do they allow Marxist professors to browbeat students who advocate Christian and conservative views?

It is abuses such as these that undermine what could and should be a valid, helpful concept. An example of the tyranny of Marxist faculties is their nefarious machinations to make academic freedom mean agreeing with them. As a result, academic freedom—instead of protecting Christian and conservative students—has morphed into one more weapon for suppressing their views.

CHAPTER 3

HISTORICAL REVISIONISM: DECEPTION, DIVISION, AND DISTORTION BY MARXIST PROFESSORS

Americans are notorious for their ignorance of U.S. history—a sad fact making it easy for Marxist professors to deny our country's Christian heritage. This is why it is important for Americans who believe in the vision of our Founders to learn our nation's true history and embrace it. When you examine the unaltered historical record, what becomes undeniably clear is the United States of America was founded by Christians and built on a solid foundation of biblical principles and Christian values.

Half of the fifty-six men who signed the Declaration of Independence held degrees from institutions affiliated with Christian churches. The Declaration contains several explicit references to God. In the first paragraph of the document are the words: ". . . to which the Laws of Nature and of

Nature's God entitle them . . ." The second paragraph contains the statement, ". . . all men are created equal, that they are endowed by their Creator with certain unalienable Rights . . ." The last sentence states, "And for the support of this Declaration, with a firm Reliance on the Protection of divine Providence, we mutually pledge to each other our Lives, our Fortunes, and our sacred Honor. . ."[1]

Evidence of America's Christian heritage is so deeply embedded in the historical record that those who reject God have found it necessary to deny, alter, conceal, and even erase that record. In so doing, they are guilty of deception, distortion, and deceit. Because Marxists who reject God have engaged in historical revisionism, students in elementary, high school, and college have, for decades, been taught a false version of America's history and heritage.

As a result, few Americans—including believers—know the truth about our country's Christian heritage. A lot of Americans have been indoctrinated in the beliefs of Marxism and secular humanism rather than being educated in truth. This is a travesty. Americans who want to play a positive role in restoring the integrity of higher education need to know the complete, unaltered history of our nation.

Americans who have not learned the truth about our country's Christian heritage need to know they have been cheated by Marxist educators who claim to have their best interests at heart but, in reality, have used them to advance an anti-Christian, anti-Conservative, anti-America agenda. But first it is important to understand Marxism as a concept and why its advocates are so determined to alter the historical record.

WHAT IS MARXISM?

If you are going to stand up to and speak out against Marxism in higher education, you need to have a solid grasp of the concept. Marxism is a sociopolitical, socioeconomic theory purporting to create a Utopian society free of class distinctions. In a Marxist society, you theoretically eliminate poor versus rich, blue-collar versus white collar, and other societal distinctions such as working poor, middle-class, and upper-class. In a Marxist society, everyone is supposed to be equal and everyone is supposed to do their part in working for the good of the overall group. In its application, Marxism is socialism with a tendency to morph into communism.

To some, Marxism sounds good in theory. After all, Marxists claim the government will provide everything the people need. Healthcare will be free, education will be free, everyone will have a job, and everyone will get an equal share of the pie. But there are at least three major problems with the concept. First, the promise of a nanny government providing for all of the people's needs is a lie; it doesn't work. Government attempts to give citizens a free life just leads to exorbitant, ever-increasing taxes and, when even high taxes aren't enough to fulfill the false promises, the government inevitably resorts to printing more and more money. Printing money irresponsibly, of course, leads to hyperinflation and just makes matters worse. This is why chronic shortages of everyday necessities are always a problem in Marxist/socialist countries—a reality America is living as we write this book.

Second, Marxism/socialism is antithetical to human nature. Not only are people not equal, except in the eyes of God, they don't want to be. People talk a lot about equality, but in reality, they want to be better, bigger, smarter, prettier, wealthier, taller, slimmer, faster, stronger, better educated, more talented, more powerful, more popular, and more secure than other people. Further, people differ vastly in such areas as physical ability, mental ability, motivation, ambition, talent, work ethic, education, perseverance, vision, and other characteristics affecting the contributions they can make to society and the success they can experience as individuals. Finally, because people want to improve their lives, they respond to incentives and the everyone-must-be-equal principle of Marxism/socialism eliminates incentives.

Because it runs counter to human nature, Marxism has failed everywhere it has been tried. Rather than remove social classes, it actually divides society into two classes: 1) those who run the government and their oligarch cronies and 2) everyone else. Top government officials are the elite in a Marxist/socialist society. Because they control everything, they get the best homes, cars, clothes, food, and amenities of life. Everyone else has to scramble for what is left. This is why the most common complaint against Marxism/socialism is that it creates a situation in which the people are equal, but only in their shared misery and lack of life's essentials.

Because its proponents ignore the exigencies of human nature, Marxism/socialism suffers from a number of inherent weaknesses contributing to its predictable failure. Prominent among these weaknesses are the following:

- Encourages government corruption and tyranny
- Breeds laziness and an entitlement mentality
- Is grounded in economic illiteracy
- Rejects the values leading to high performance, productivity, creativity, and innovation
- Indoctrinates rather than educates
- Is intolerant of dissenting views

These weaknesses are why Marxism/socialism failed in the Soviet Union, Cuba, and the Scandinavian countries that tried it and had to return to capitalism. This is also why it is now failing in Venezuela. Marxism/socialism fares no better in China. The only reason China has become an economic powerhouse is the Chinese Communist Party established free-market enterprise zones that are now cash cows propping up the nation's government. In other words, to survive as a Marxist/socialist/communist nation, China had to resort to capitalism.

The third and greatest weakness of Marxism/socialism—the one leading to all others—is its rejection of the God of Holy Scripture. The religion of Marxists is secular humanism, atheism, or agnosticism (see chapter 6). All these religions worship the god of self which makes them diametrically opposed to Christianity. This being the case, Marxists believe they must systematically remove Christianity from the culture. Doing so is accomplished by removing the Bible, prayer, Christian symbols, and Christian influence from a nation's institutions, the public square, and ultimately all aspects of daily life. The process can be viewed in microcosm by observing what is taking place on the campuses of colleges and universities nationwide.

It is ironic how Marxists have gained a foothold in America. Our country's Founders were guided in every instance by biblical principles in the deliberations, decisions, and actions that led to the establishment of our nation. However, in the America of today Marxists reject any kind of Christian influence in matters of government, public policy, education, and daily life. This is why they find it necessary to deny, distort, and revise the historical record. For this reason, it is important for Christians and Conservatives to understand the truth about America's Christian heritage.

IRREFUTABLE EVIDENCE OF AMERICA'S CHRISTIAN HERITAGE

No serious, honest student of history would deny our America's Christian heritage. The evidence is too conclusive, too persuasive, and ubiquitous. Even a cursory review of the unaltered historical record reveals mountains of corroborating evidence. This evidence can be found in the writings of America's early settlers, inscriptions carved in stone in our nation's capital, the proceedings of the Continental Congress, the religious affiliations of America's first colleges, and the words of our Founding Fathers, presidents, supreme court justices, congressional reports, and original state constitutions.

What follows in the remainder of this chapter is a summary of some of the most easily accessible evidence from the historical record. This summary only scratches the surface of what is available to anyone interested in knowing the truth rather than denying or distorting it. However, Americans who know only what follows in this chapter will have plenty of evidence for refuting the false claims of those who deny our country's Christian heritage.

Evidence from America's Early European Settlers

Some of America's earliest European settlers were the Pilgrims who left their homelands seeking religious freedom. Tired of being forced to accept the religion mandated by European monarchs or suffer persecution for refusing, the Pilgrims banded together and risked everything to start new lives on a new continent. They sailed on a tiny ship—the *Mayflower*—across the Atlantic Ocean to North America with the intention of landing on the coast of Virginia. Every man and woman on board the *Mayflower* was determined to begin a new life and practice his or her own religion without interference, coercion, or persecution from kings, queens, or their minions.

After a rough voyage in which they were blown well off course, the Pilgrims anchored offshore from Plymouth, well north of their intended destination. Nevertheless, these intrepid Pilgrims decided they would start their new lives where God planted them. Their landing place became Plymouth Colony, then Massachusetts Bay Colony, and eventually the state of Massachusetts. Their first order of business was developing a governing document called the Mayflower Compact. The most important paragraph in the document reads as follows:

> Having undertaken for the glory of God, and advancement of the Christian faith, and honor of our king and country, a voyage to plant the first colony in the northern parts of Virginia, do by these presents solemnly and mutually, in the presence of God, and one another, covenant and combine our selves together into a civil body politic. . .[2]

One can easily see why secular authors and publishers either censor this portion of the Mayflower Compact or leave the entire document out of history books. The Mayflower Compact leaves no doubt about where the early European settlers stood on Christianity. It also makes their intentions in settling in America crystal clear. Their plan was to advance the Christian faith and plant a colony in North America governed according to biblical principles.

Although they were well off course in reaching their planned destination, they were right on course when it came to building a colony on a foundation of Christianity. The Pilgrims sought neither fame nor fortune. Rather, they sought to honor God and secure religious freedom for themselves and their families. The Mayflower Compact is just one example of many in which the truth requires secularists to engage in historical revisionism.

Evidence from Inscriptions Carved in Stone in Our Nation's Capital

If you visit our nation's capital, Washington, D.C., you will find abundant evidence of America's Christian heritage. In fact, you will be surrounded by it. References to God are ubiquitous throughout the capital. Washington, D.C. presents a real challenge to historical revisionists because it contains evidence not easily erased since it is carved in stone. Let's look at just four of the more popular stops on a tour of our nation's capital: the Washington Monument, Lincoln Memorial, Jefferson Memorial, and Capitol.

Climbing the stairs in the Washington Monument you will find such phrases as "Holiness to the Lord," "Search the Scriptures," and "In God We Trust" inscribed there. Visit the Lincoln Memorial and you will find these words from the 16th president's Gettysburg Address: "We here highly resolve that these dead shall not have died in vain, that this nation, under God, shall have a new birth of freedom." Lincoln's second inaugural address is also inscribed on the wall of the monument. This address is filled with references to God, fourteen in all.

The Jefferson Memorial also contains numerous references to God. For example, the following words are inscribed on the dome of the monument: "I have sworn on the altar of God, eternal hostility against every form of tyranny over the mind of man." On the wall of the monument, you will find Jefferson's best-known lines from the Declaration of Independence: "We hold these truths to be self-evident: That all men are created equal, that they are endowed by their Creator with certain unalienable rights, that among these are life, liberty, and the pursuit of happiness."

The Capitol—the very symbol of republican self-government—is replete with references to God. Several paintings in the Rotunda of the Capitol depict Christian scenes. The phrase "In God We Trust" is carved into the wall above the Speaker's rostrum in the House of Representatives. Inscribed at the east entrance of the Senate Chamber are the words "Annuit Coeptis." This phrase is Latin for God has favored our undertakings. The words "In

God We Trust" are inscribed at the southern entrance of the Senate Chamber.

The few inscriptions mentioned here are just the tip of an extensive iceberg. One could fill a notebook with the references to God and Christianity carved in stone in Washington, D.C. No objective person can visit our nation's capital and thereafter deny the reality of America's Christian heritage. Historical revisionists are not objective. They have an agenda that excludes God. They must, therefore, deny, distort, and alter the historical record.

Evidence from the Proceedings of the Continental Congress

The Continental Congress first convened on September 5, 1774. Prior to taking any action, the members invoked the blessings of God on the historic and unprecedented task they were about to undertake. The first official act of the Conti nental Congress was passing a resolution requiring the proceedings of the body to be opened with prayer. The prayer was offered by a local pastor who also read the 31st Psalm to the members. This passage of Scripture contains the following words: "Be strong and let your hearts take courage, all you who wait on the Lord."

Having asked the Lord to bless their work, the delegates set to work developing the Articles of Confederation, a precursor to the Constitution. The Articles of Confederation served as America's guiding document until nine of the thirteen colonies later ratified the Constitution. In dating the final version of the Articles, the delegates wrote the following phrase: ". . . in the year of our Lord one Thousand seven Hundred and Seventy-eight. . ."[3] There is no question the Continental Congress was composed of Christians who knew their Bible and acted in accordance with its teachings.

Evidence from America's Earliest Colleges

It is sad and even ironic that, for the most part, institutions of higher education in this country have become ardent opponents of Christianity. It would be difficult to find a place less friendly to Christians than the typical university campus. America's institutions of higher education have become incubators for American Marxism, hotbeds of Leftist activism, and re-education centers for socialist indoctrination. As a result, Christian beliefs are not just rejected by elitist Marxist professors, they are often ridiculed and, in some cases, forbidden. Christian students are frequently belittled and sometimes persecuted. Christian speakers are often denied invitations or when invited shouted down by secular activists.

The reason the anti-God attitude permeates higher education in America is sad and self-evident, but why is it ironic? It is ironic because, as shown in chapter 2, America's earliest colleges were founded by believers for the purpose of promulgating Christianity. Most graduates of these early institutions received religion-related degrees. All graduates of these institutions were well-schooled in biblical teachings. Students who did not know their Bible did not graduate from America's earliest colleges.

The Marxist ideologues who now control higher education in America have done everything possible to hide and paint over the Christian visions of our Founders. For example, the original motto of Harvard College was *Veritas Christo et Ecclesiae* which is Latin for "Truth for Christ and the Church."[4] This motto was chiseled in stone in the archway over the entrance to Harvard yard. This motto has since been reduced to just one word: *Veritas*, which is Latin for truth.[5] The truth these days is Harvard is opposed to God and the truth.

The problem with Harvard's scaled-down motto is the use of the word "truth." The institution originally acknowledged the Bible as the source of truth, but that is no longer the case. Rather, the prevailing philosophy at Harvard, as at most universities in America, is either atheism or secular humanism. A good working definition for an atheist is a person who does not believe in God and is mad at him. A good working definition for a secular humanist is someone who thinks he or she is god, as we explain in chapter 6.

A guiding principle of secular humanism and atheism is moral relativism. Moral relativists claim there is no such thing as absolute truth. To a secular humanist, moral absolutes do not exist. Rather, truth, as well as right and wrong, are determined by the individual. Carry this belief out to its logical conclusion and the undeniable but troublesome result is every individual is his or her own god. Small wonder, then, there is so much disagreement, discord, and dissention in the anti-God community.

With secular humanists and atheists, who decides what is right when they—all of them their own little god—disagree? One could drive a truck through the holes in the logic of moral relativism and atheism. For example, to claim there are no absolutes—as do secular humanists and atheists—is to state an absolute. Secular humanists and atheists believe man is capable of navigating through life without any help from God by applying human logic, reason, and common sense, but it is these very factors that make the concept self-refuting. Few people other than the character, Spock, in the old television series, *Star Trek*, are consistently logical or reasonable, and common sense is hardly common. In fact, it is one of the rarest of human characteristics.

Evidence from the Founding Fathers

The words of the Founding Fathers, written and spoken, leave no doubt as to their Christian beliefs. One could fill a book the size of the Oxford English Dictionary with the faith-related statements of our Founders. The few statements summarized herein are representative but not comprehensive. There are thousands more like them in the historical record.

People who were educated before the days of historical revisionism are familiar with the famous words of Patrick Henry: "I know not what course others may take, but as for me, give me liberty or give me death."[6] Fewer people know the statements preceding these words. Leading up to his well-known remark, Patrick Henry made clear his reliance and that of his compatriots on God.

Henry was speaking to the Second Virginia Convention on March 23, 1775, when he proclaimed: "An appeal to arms and to the God of hosts is all that is left to us! . . . Sir, we are not weak if we make a proper use of those means which the God of nature hath placed in our power. . . . There is a just God who presides over the destinies of nations. . . . Is life so dear, or peace so sweet as to be purchased at the price of chains and slavery? Forbid it, Almighty God!"[7] Only after this powerful lead-in did Henry make his now famous remark.

One of the best-known Founding Fathers, Benjamin Franklin, may have saved our fledgling nation from failing before it got started by reminding his fellow delegates to the Constitutional Convention of the words in Psalm 127:1. It was May 1787. General Washington and his citizen soldiers had finally defeated the British. The next challenge faced by the Founders was developing a blueprint for transforming the idea of the United States of America into reality. That blueprint was the Constitution.

Delegates from the various states met in Philadelphia to hammer out the details included in the Constitution, a document that would serve as a *user's manual* for governing the new nation and turning the philosophical ideals stated in the Declaration of Independence into practical policies. But things weren't going well. The delegates were deeply divided over a host of issues. Tempers flared, collegiality evaporated, and courtesy gave way to angry recriminations.

It was at this point that an aged and ailing Benjamin Franklin took the floor and made the following statement:

> I have lived, sir, a long time, and the longer I live, the more convincing proofs I see of this truth: that God governs in the affairs of men. And if a sparrow cannot fall to the ground without His notice, is it probable that an empire can rise without His aid? We have been assured, sir, in the sacred writings that "except the Lord builds the house, they labor in vain who build it." I firmly believe this; and I also believe without His concurring aid we shall succeed in this political building no better than the builders of Babel.[8]

These were powerful words coming from a man who was widely respected by his fellow Founders. But Franklin's words are even more powerful today because historical revisionists like to claim he was a deist rather than a Christian. To review, deists reject the existence of a supernatural creator who governs in the everyday lives of men. Franklin's statement made at the Constitutional Convention in May 1787 are not the words of a deist. Rather, they are the words of a man who clearly believed God governs in the everyday lives of His children. Perhaps at the end of his life Franklin saw his beliefs more clearly as often happens as people age. However, regardless one's views on Franklin's religious beliefs, on at least one day in May 1787 he spoke the words of a true believer.

Thomas Jefferson, America's third president and principal author of the Declaration of Independence, is another Founder historical revisionists claim was a deist rather than a Christian. Judge for yourself if his words are the words of a man who believed God created the world and then turned His back on it leaving His children to fend for themselves: ". . . can the liberties of a nation be thought secure when we have removed their only firm basis, a conviction in the minds of the people that these liberties are the gift of God? That they are not to be violated but with his wrath? Indeed, I tremble for my country when I reflect that God is just: that his justice cannot sleep forever."[9] Jefferson's are hardly the words of a deist. If God does not involve Himself in the everyday lives of man, there is nothing to tremble about.

Jefferson's words are enshrined forever on the wall of the Jefferson Memorial in Washington, D.C., as are several other quotes with clear and purposeful references to the God of Holy Scripture. The words inscribed on the walls and dome of the Jefferson Memorial are not the words of a deist. Rather, they are the words of a Founding Father who looked to God and His Word for guidance in establishing and governing a new nation: the United States of America.

Evidence from the Words of U.S. Presidents

Further evidence of America's Christian heritage can be found in the words of our nation's early chief executives, the ones who helped establish our country. Presidents of the United States set the tone for our country by the words they speak. One can learn much about the United States by studying their words. Try this experiment. Assume you are a person who knows nothing about the United States. Read the words from the former presidents quoted in the following paragraphs and then ask yourself this question: What conclusions can I draw concerning the United States from these statements?

In his Thanksgiving Proclamation on October 3, 1789, George Washington, America's first president said: "It is the duty of all nations to acknowledge the providence of Almighty God, to obey his will, to be grateful for his benefits, and humbly to implore his protection and favor."[10] Speaking to the Massachusetts militia on October 11, 1798, Washington's successor, John Adams, made the following statement: "Our Constitution was made only for a moral and religious People. It is wholly inadequate to the government of any other."[11]

James Monroe was America's fifth president. In his State of the Union address on November 16, 1818, Monroe made the following statement: "When we view the blessings with which our country has been favored, those which we now enjoy, and the means which we possess of handing them down unimpaired to our latest posterity, our attention is drawn to the source from whence they flow. Let us then, unite on offering our most grateful acknowledgments for these blessings to the Divine Author of All Good."[12]

Now, return to the experiment suggested at the beginning of this section. If you knew nothing about America, what would you learn from reviewing the words of these early presidents? The one thing you would know for certain is America was founded on Christian principles by individuals who not only believed in God but looked to Him for guidance in performing the duties of the presidency. In other words, you would learn America has a strong Christian heritage.

Evidence from Supreme Court Justices and Rulings

In rendering their opinions and commenting on cases brought before the bench, early Supreme Court Justices left behind a mountain of evidence concerning America's Christian heritage. For example, in a unanimous decision in *Church of the Holy Trinity v. U.S.* (1892), the Justices stated: "These, and many other matters which might be noticed, add a volume of unofficial declarations to the mass of organic utterances that this is a Christian nation."[13]

John Jay, the first Chief Justice of the Supreme Court, made clear his views on America's Christian heritage. On October 12, 1816, he said: "Providence has given to our people the choice of their rulers, and it is the duty, as well as the privilege and interest of our Christian nation, to select and prefer Christians for their rulers."[14] In a letter to Peter Augustus Jay, his eldest son, dated April 9, 1784, John Jay wrote: "The Bible is the best of all books, for it is the word of God and teaches us the way to be happy in this world and in the next. Continue therefore to read it and to regulate your life by its precepts."[15]

In *The Works of the Honourable James Wilson*, one of the six original Supreme Court Justices states: "Human law must rest its authority ultimately upon the authority of that law which is divine. Far from being rivals or enemies, religion and law are twin sisters, friends, and mutual assistance."[16] Clearly, more recent Justices have ignored their own principle of following judicial precedent when deciding cases.

In *Vidal v. Girard's Executors* (1844), the Supreme Court issued a unanimous decision supporting the use of the Bible in public schools. Their decision contained the following statement: "Why may not the Bible, and especially the New Testament, without note or comment, be read and taught as a divine revelation in (schools)—its general precepts expounded, its evidence explained and its glorious principles inculcated? Where can the principles of morality be learned so clearly or so perfectly as from the New Testament?"[17]

These few examples, though not comprehensive, are representative of the statements of early Supreme Court Justices and Supreme Court decisions. In fact, until 1947 all precedents from the Supreme Court were supportive of Christianity. They also reinforced the fact the United States was founded on biblical principles and Christian values. When the

Supreme Court handed down its "separation of church and state" decision in 1947, the Justices ignored more than 150 years of legal precedent and, at the same time, established a new precedent: legislating from the bench. The Supreme Court is supposed to rule on the Constitutionality of laws passed by Congress, not create new laws. Legislating from the bench is judicial usurpation and it continues to this day.

Evidence from Congressional Reports

There is little evidence of America's Christian heritage in the recorded proceedings of Congress today, but this wasn't always the case. Committee reports from a different era in Congress demonstrate clearly that America was founded as a Christian nation. For example, a report from the Senate Judiciary Committee dated January 19, 1853, reads in part as follows: "We are a Christian people . . . not because the law demands it, not to gain exclusive benefits or to avoid legal disabilities, but from choice and education; and in a land thus universally Christian, what is to be expected, what desired, but that we shall pay due regard to Christianity?"[18]

This report makes the important point that Americans were Christians at the time by choice and education. Nobody forced them to accept Christianity; America was not a theocracy. Americans at this time in our nation's history choose to be Christians and built the teaching of Christianity into the education of their children. This is important because atheists and secular humanists have succeeded in removing the teaching of Christianity from all forms of education except Christian schools. It's not just that children who attend public schools in America today are no longer taught Christian principles; they are taught just the opposite no matter what their parents believe.

The House Judiciary Committee issued a report on March 27, 1854: "At the time of the adoption of the

Constitution and the amendments, the universal sentiment was that Christianity should be encouraged. . . . In this age there can be no substitute for Christianity. . . . That was the religion of the founders and the republic and they expected it to remain the religion of their descendants."[19]

This report makes it clear: Christianity was the religion of the Founders. They were not atheists, agnostics, or deists as secular humanists like to claim. They were Christians. Further, the Founders were not just Christians; they expected their descendants to be Christians. Christianity was to be "encouraged" not belittled, suppressed, and banned as it is in the public schools, colleges and universities, and public square today.

Evidence from the Original State Constitutions

The individual states comprising the United States of America have their own state constitutions. Although Leftist ideologues have succeeded in radically altering these documents over the years, the original state constitutions demonstrate beyond the slightest doubt that America was founded as a Christian nation. Let's consider the original constitutions of two states, one from the north and one from the south. These two state constitutions are not unique. Rather, they are representative of all the original state constitutions.

The original state constitution of Massachusetts (circa 1780) was written in part by native son and second president of the United States, John Adams. The Massachusetts constitution at that time required all elected officials to take an oath in which they swore not just that Christianity represents the truth but that they were Christians who accepted and believed the tenets of the religion.[20]

The original state constitution of South Carolina (circa 1778) contained five points which demonstrated clearly that

America was founded as a Christian nation. These five points are as follows:

1. There is only one God and God is eternal.
2. The God of Holy Scripture should be worshipped publicly.
3. There is only one true religion and that religion is Christianity.
4. The Bible is the divinely-inspired Word of God and, as such, it should govern both faith and daily life.
5. Every man is required to bear witness to the truth, the source of which is the Christian Bible.[21]

The evidence of America's Christian heritage presented herein only scratches the surface of what is readily available to anyone who is interested in knowing the true, unaltered history of our country. Unfortunately, the true and unaltered history of our country is no longer taught in public schools or colleges and universities. Because of this, students of all ages are being taught a false and destructive picture of what America stands for and what it means to be an American. This is why it is important you to learn the truth about America's Christian heritage, make sure your children learn it, and insist it be taught in the schools they attend regardless of whether those schools are public, private, or Christian.

We are not advocating a state-enforced religion, for no such thing is possible. We want America's founding to be taught truthfully in public education so the biblical principles it establishes and maintains can once again pervade our culture and government.

CHAPTER 4

"IDENTITY DEGREES" AND THE DUMBING DOWN OF HIGHER EDUCATION

Since the 1960s, colleges and universities have introduced a number of politically correct, woke college degrees with at least two unfortunate characteristics in common: they lack academic rigor and are unmarketable in the real world. Traditionally, college degrees have opened opportunities for graduates because, as a result of their studies, they are better prepared than non-graduates to be productive, contributing citizens and leaders of organizations, communities, states, and the nation.

Students with college degrees have traditionally been able to earn more money, enjoy better career opportunities, benefit from better job security, enjoy higher levels of job satisfaction, and demand better perks and benefits than non-college graduates. This is still the case for students who select high-demand, marketable college degrees. However, more and more students who are incapable of pursuing academically demanding degrees or are disinclined to put forth the necessary effort are enrolling in programs that do little more than turn them into habitually offended snowflakes who view themselves as victims. These poor-me programs equip students to be nothing more than unemployed and perpetually angry Marxist minions.

The worst of the poor-me college majors are known as "identity degrees." These programs are so disconnected from the real world as to be unmarketable and of questionable value outside the fantasyland of a college or university campus. Yet, increasingly students are enrolling in these identity programs and spending $200,000 or more—often borrowed money—on degrees with no more value than their high-school diplomas. In fact, it is not uncommon for a bachelor's degree to cost more than $400,000 when tuition, fees, books, and room and board are factored in (see chapter 5).

One cannot help but question the judgment of counselors who encourage students to pursue worthless identity degrees. Why would students spend so much money pursuing degrees with so little value? Why spend so much money pursuing a degree that will leave them burdened with lifelong debt they have no hope of paying off? It's like paying thousands of dollars for a broken-down car that doesn't run and never will.

Colleges and universities like to claim their graduates typically earn greater than 80 percent over the course of a lifetime than high school graduates. What they don't tell potential students is this kind of earning potential applies only to a limited number of degrees. These high-value college majors include engineering, science, math, healthcare, quality management, and safety management degrees. They don't include the low-value, feel-good, identity degrees being propagated by Marxist professors.

IDENTITY DEGREES

Up until the 1960s, there was a direct correlation between what college students majored in and the level of demand for their degrees. The most popular college degrees were in academic disciplines needed by society, disciplines corresponding to high-demand fields in the real world. Some still are. But high-demand fields are high-demand because only a limited number of students are able to handle the academic rigor associated with them. This is why universities have had to spread their nets wider and recruit foreign students to maintain their enrollments in such disciples as science, technology, engineering, and math, the STEM disciplines.

As Marxist indoctrination and dumbing down in the K-12 school system worked together to limit even further the number of students capable of succeeding in these traditional high-demand degree programs, colleges and universities had to do something to shore up their enrollments. Sensing an opportunity to kill two birds with one stone, Marxist professors and administrators responded by introducing—one might say inventing—minimally challenging programs even underprepared students who probably don't belong in college in the first place can navigate. Provided, of course, they can pay the tuition. These programs serve to shore up enrollments while, at the same time, serving as launching pads for successive generations of newly minted Marxists.

The more popular of these identity programs, invented by Marxist ideologues, include Women's Studies, Queer Studies, LGBTQ Studies, Transgender Studies, Black Studies, Chicano/Latino Studies, Native American Studies, and Fat Studies. In fact, a good rule of thumb is to be suspicious of any college degree program using the term "studies" in its title. That word, when attached to the title of a degree program, typically means there is no corresponding profession associated with the program in the real world. Try this experiment. Check any job listings and see if you can find any stating, "We are looking for graduates of Women's Studies, Queer Studies, LGBTQ Studies, Transgender Studies, Black Studies, Chicano/Latino Studies, Native American Studies, and Fat Studies Programs."

All of these identity degree programs share a common but unstated purpose: to convince students they are a repressed minority, misunderstood and mistreated by the world and entitled to sympathy if not compensation. Students in these programs learn to feel good about themselves but angry and resentful toward everyone else. Identity programs promote a tribal mentality, an us-against-the-world attitude in which students are taught to view themselves as entitled victims.

Classes taught in identity programs come closer to resembling therapy sessions than legitimate college work. Rather than helping students develop marketable knowledge and skills, these programs teach students to be suspicious of everyone else in society who is of a different identity. For the purpose of illustration, let's look at just two identity programs; the largest and most-widely offered of them (Women's Studies) and the strangest of them (Fat Studies).

Example 1: Women's Studies

What do students learn in a Women's Studies program? A review of college catalogues reveals the typical Women's Study curriculum is designed to help students learn the following: What it means to be a woman, how gender roles influence one's experience as a woman or man, how gender roles have changed over the years, the basics of feminism, and the politics of women.

Typical courses taken in a Women's Studies program include Overview of Sexual Minorities, History of Sexuality,

Gender and Society, Feminist Theory, and Feminism and Public Policy. Notice the built-in bias in these programs. They are called Women's Studies, but they cater to feminists, thereby excluding a large percentage of the women in America. For example, mothers who stay home and raise children and women who work but reject the political agenda of feminism would be out of place in these programs. These are not really programs of study for women. Rather, they are programs for Leftist/Marxist women.

Further, what women supposedly learn in these programs could be taught in just one elective course. There is hardly sufficient academic content in these programs to warrant four years of college study. Worse yet, when women complete this kind of program, what do they have? What have they gotten for their money? Where is the return on investment? Let us assume women who complete this kind of program know everything there is to know about sexual minorities, the history of sexuality, gender and society, feminist theory, and feminism and public policy. Where does that leave them once they take off their cap and gown? Where do they go and what do they do with that knowledge? The marketplace is hardly crying out for people with this kind of knowledge.

Example 2: Fat Studies

Fat Studies programs may be the best example of higher education straying from its stated purpose to advance a Marxist agenda. Does an overweight individual really need a four-year degree to understand how it feels to be fat? The overall theme of Fat Studies programs is it's perfectly acceptable to be fat. Students in these programs learn they are victims of an insensitive society and, as a result, should push back against anyone who questions that assertion, including physicians who are concerned about the well-documented health ramifications of obesity. Fat Studies students learn about such supposed concepts as *fat oppression, sizeism, fat shaming,* and *body bias.*

Fat Studies programs actually teach students that being fat is not unhealthy in spite of mountains of scientific evidence to the contrary, evidence clearly showing the correlations between weight and blood pressure, heart attacks, strokes, and diabetes. However, in Fat Studies programs, physicians who recommend obese patients lose weight are considered insensitive louts who harbor deep-seated prejudices learned from living in a society biased against fat people.

The problems with Fat Studies programs are manifest. These programs amount to little more than a series of feel-good activities masquerading as education but wholly lacking in intellectual integrity, not to mention academic rigor. Rather than giving students solid evidence, documented knowledge, and practical skills they might use to improve their lives, these programs encourage students to view themselves as helpless victims. Worse yet, after paying the high cost of a college degree for little more than four years of feel-good therapy, what do graduates of these programs have to show for their time, effort, and money? Has anyone ever seen a job listing that reads, "We are looking for an obese individual who thinks it's okay to be fat"?

THE DUMBING DOWN OF HIGHER EDUCATION

College students once studied Latin and Greek. They are now more likely to study remedial English. College students once studied calculus. They are now more likely to study pre-algebra if they are required to study mathematics at all. A survey by the American Council of Trustees and Alumni of America's top-ranked public universities revealed only nine of them required students to take an economics course;

just five required a course in American history; only ten required a literature course; and fewer than half required a foreign language.[1]

A study sponsored by the National Endowment for the Humanities revealed how most college seniors would fail even a basic-level test on Western culture and history; 25 percent could not distinguish between the principles advocated by Karl Marx and those found in the U.S. Constitution; 42 percent could not place the Civil War in the correct half-century; most knew nothing about the Missouri Compromise, Magna Carta, or Reconstruction; and they were not familiar with such books as *Pride and Prejudice* by Jane Austen or *Crime and Punishment* by Fyodor Dostoevsky.[2]

Over the years, as the K-12 public school system in America devolved into Marxist indoctrination and mushy-headed "wokeness," fewer and fewer students graduated from high school prepared to enter college. Rather than see their enrollments decline as a result, institutions of higher education lowered their standards, began offering remedial courses, removed rigorous content from existing core courses and, worse yet, eliminated the required academic core in some cases. As a result, today's college students are able to study almost anything without necessarily learning anything.[3]

A high percentage of students are progressing through college today without making any measurable gains in general skills. Although students may be gaining a higher level of self-awareness, they are not improving in such areas as critical thinking, complex reasoning, and writing. Yet, 93 percent of employers surveyed by the Association of American Colleges and Universities stated, the ability to think critically, communicate clearly, and solve complex problems is more important than an individual's college major.[4]

Colleges and universities once required all students in all majors to complete a strong academic core including English literature, mathematics, science, history, foreign languages, and Western civilization. This academically rigorous core ensured all college graduates, no matter what they majored in, received a broad, deep, and well-rounded education.

Because of the requirement to complete a strong academic core, students who majored in a scientific discipline could converse intelligently about English literature. Correspondingly, students who majored in history could solve the quadratic equation. Having completed a rigorous academic core was considered a sign of an educated person. Unfortunately, in many institutions this strong core of required courses has been replaced by a menu of options allowing students to pick and choose their way around the more difficult courses; the ones with bona fide academic content.

Further evidence of the dumbing down of higher education can be found in the amount of class time required of students. For years the trend has been declining. The academic year has shrunk over time, as has the amount of time actually spent in class. For example, a college course that is supposed to meet for forty-five hours over the course of a semester actually meets only 37.5 hours; the academic hour has decreased to fifty minutes. Whereas classes on Saturday used to be common, on today's college or university campus classes on Friday are becoming a rarity. Here is a joke often heard on college campuses these days: What's more deserted than a church on Monday? The answer: a college campus on Friday.

Not surprisingly, college and university administrators are offended by any suggestion they have dumbed down their curriculums. They try to rationalize dumbing down by self-righteously droning on about such supposedly high-minded concepts as diversity, inclusiveness, and cultural sensitivity. According to woke administrators, the required core should be diverse enough to be of interest to a wide spectrum of students, inclusive enough that people of all races, genders, and worldviews can find courses they are comfortable with, and culturally sensitive enough students of different backgrounds aren't offended by it.

This kind of rationale sounds appealing until you realize it is pure fantasy. College and university curriculums have been dumbed down to bolster enrollments and improve student retention. The more watered down the academic requirements, the more students who can enroll and make progress rather than dropping out. Few things are more important to administrators and professors in higher education than enrollments and retention because they both result in more money. When students cannot meet the entrance requirements and when they flunk out, institutions lose money.

Whereas, in the past, students would have studied the works of Shakespeare and Chaucer, today they are just as likely to enroll in such courses as "Fat Shaming in American Society," "Gender Bias in the Workplace," "A Defense of Transgenderism," or "The Case for Socialism." There has never been a time in our nation's history when serious scholarship was needed more badly than now. There has never been a time when the United States needed well-prepared college graduates who are able to compete against their counterparts across the globe more than now.

The key to global competitiveness in today's world is brain power. Brain power is what allows college graduates to provide society what it needs so society will, in turn, abundantly compensate the graduates. College graduates cannot be contributing members of society unless they have something to contribute, something society needs.

DUMBING DOWN OF EDUCATION IS A NATIONAL SECURITY ISSUE

The dumbing down of education at all levels is creating a national security crisis. The quality of the U.S. military is at risk because 30 percent of today's high school graduates cannot pass the Armed Forces Qualification Tests.[5] Worse yet, while foreign college students are majoring in such academic disciplines as engineering, science, and technology, American students are pursuing feel-good identity degrees.

While foreign students in American universities are learning how to hack into and disable America's electrical grid and computer-controlled systems, U.S. students are sitting through little more than amateur therapy sessions. While foreign students are learning to do things useful and helpful to society, American students are being transformed into Leftist snowflakes who are offended by anything requiring intelligence or effort.

Universities argue that their science, technology, engineering, and math (STEM) programs are full to the brim with students. However, what they don't admit is most of the enrollees in these disciplines are foreign students who will take their college degrees back to their countries of origin and use them there rather than in the United States and, in many cases, against the United States. For example, approximately 60 percent of all foreign students in American universities are enrolled in science and engineering fields. Most of these come from India or China.[6] What is ironic in this is woke American students will not be coddled and catered to by real Marxists such as the Chinese should they emerge victorious in their vision of world conquest.

If American universities did not enroll foreign students in their STEM programs, they would have too few students to justify offering these programs. Another reason universities covet foreign students is money. Tuition for foreign students is much higher than for American students, often five times higher. In other words, American universities are selling their own country down the river for the sake of the almighty dollar. It is ironic, though not surprising, that Marxists/socialists would be so interested in the almighty dollar.

The United States can continue to compete on the global stage only if it produces high school and college graduates who can outthink, out-innovate, and outwork their counterparts in other countries. Dumbing down the education system produces the opposite result. The American military can continue to defend our country only if it can attract high school and college graduates who are smarter, better at critical thinking, and faster learners than their counterparts in other countries. Dumbing down the education system produces the opposite result.

Writing for *Forbes* magazine, Arthur Herman summarized the national security implications of dumbing down education comprehensively but succinctly: "A future shortfall in Americans trained in science and engineering bodes ill not only for our economic well-being, but for our national security as well. This is because so many current and future defense systems will depend on technologies in which America still leads in development and innovation, such as cyber, artificial intelligence, quantum research, and even nanotechnology—but where competitors are pushing hard to overtake us and dominate the high-tech future."[7]

The solution to our growing national security threat is for education at all levels to reverse the dumbing-down process and replace Marxist indoctrination with high-quality education (more about that in chapter 8). In the short term, the fastest and most effective way to increase the number of American students majoring in academic disciplines needed in the marketplace and by society in general is to make government-backed student loans available only to students who enroll in these high-demand, high-priority programs for which there is a legitimate national need. Do this and government-backed student loans will be an investment in America's future instead of a way for students to waste four or more years pursuing degrees with the market value of polluted water.

If students want to pursue identity degrees or degrees in other fields of study with no value in the marketplace and that serve no high-priority national interest, fine; but let them pay their own way. Why should American taxpayers underwrite the exorbitant costs associated with college degrees when those degrees do little or nothing to improve America's economic well-being, national defense, or cultural quality?

CHAPTER 5

THE HIGH COSTS OF A COLLEGE DEGREE AND THE STUDENT LOAN DEBACLE

Going to college is a costly endeavor. In fact, it is one of the more costly ventures most people will ever undertake. Pursing a college degree costs students in two ways. The most obvious costs are financial. Completing a four-year degree becomes more expensive every year. Further, unless students are wise about the degrees they pursue, the return on investment will fall short of the amount invested. In many cases there is no return on investment. Pursuing certain woke college majors amounts to throwing money down the drain.

Second, and more important, pursuing a college degree can cost students by changing who they are as human beings. Four years of study under Marxist professors can alter a student's values, beliefs, and worldview. Many students end up selling their souls to complete a college degree. Of course, this is precisely what Marxist professors want. They view your sons and daughters as raw material to be molded, shaped, and transformed into the Marxist ideologues of tomorrow. To a great extent, America's future is in the hands of today's college students. Marxist ideologues hope to control that future by remolding your sons and daughters in their image. In this chapter, we look at the financial and personal costs of a college degree as well as the added costs associated with student loans. First, the potential personal cost of a college education.

POTENTIAL PERSONAL COSTS OF A COLLEGE DEGREE

Mark 8:36 is a precautionary verse from Scripture with direct application for young people considering college. This verse reads: "For what does it profit a man to gain the whole world and forfeit his soul?" An apt paraphrase of this verse is: For what does it profit students to gain a college degree and forfeit how God made them? Losing one's soul is the ultimate potential personal cost of a college degree. In chapter 8, we explain how Christian and conservative students can earn college degrees without losing their souls. In this chapter, we discuss the potential personal costs of spending four or more years under the nefarious tutelage of Marxist professors.

We can no longer count the number of times we have heard frustrated parents claim, "Since they went away to college, we don't even recognize our children." If the college experience is approached without the proper caution and determination needed to stay grounded in their fundamental beliefs, college students can find themselves being transformed into individuals their parents, pastors, and friends no longer know. They leave home as young warriors in the army of God and American patriots. Four years later they return as Leftist ideologues who hate America, reject God, and sneer at their parents' values.

Jordan Peterson has emerged as a popular and powerful proponent of traditional values and opponent of woke ideology. In one of his website blog posts, he recalls his experience on modern college campuses reflecting the radicalization of students:

> I've had highly stressful experiences at the University of Toronto, McMaster and Queen's and elsewhere in the recent past, when I was confronted by mobs of misbehaving activists, agitated by their ideologically-possessed professors, blaring air horns at distances close enough to cause permanent hearing damage, and chanting slogans which they did not even take the time to craft into rhythm. At Queen's, most infamously, about 150 protesters surrounded the rather church-like edifice in which I was speaking, along with Dr. Bruce Pardy, of Queen's Law School. Dozens of them climbed onto the sills of the old ten-foot stained glass windows that lined the outer walls and pounded continuously on them for the full 90 minutes of the talk. One such luminary, later arrested with a garrotte (!), performed her services with enough force to break a window and smear it with blood. Outside, the self-styled heroes of the new revolution barricaded the exterior doors—a crime, by the way—and humorously suggested that burning the building down, with all the attendees and speakers inside, might constitute an acceptable way to proceed.[1]

Granted, Peterson comes from the Canadian academy, but the examples he uses are not divergent from the American experience. If anything, Canada gives us a view to the future if rampant socialist indoctrination in our education is not stopped.

Marxist professors not only reject traditional American (Western civilizational) values, they work hard to supplant them with the "values" of socialism. With socialism, capitalism is replaced by collectivism in which the government controls every aspect of daily life, individualism is replaced by government-enforced group think, free speech is replaced by government mandated political correctness, American exceptionalism is replaced by an I-hate-America attitude, self-reliance is replaced by the entitlement mentality, and the morality of wealth creation is replaced by taxation so exorbitantly high it kills initiative, creativity, and entrepreneurship.

The financial costs associated with a college degree are unjustifiably high and increasing rapidly. However, these kinds of costs pale in comparison to the personal costs many students and their families pay for pursuing college degrees. This being the case, we encourage parents with children approaching college age to dig deep into chapter 8 of this book and take to heart what is recommended there.

FINANCIAL COSTS OF A COLLEGE DEGREE

The Marxist ideologues who control higher education lobby Congress constantly and persistently to enact "free" college tuition nationwide, an appealing idea to a lot of Americans with children approaching college age. Because of its appeal, Joe Biden made it part of his political platform, borrowed from avowed socialist, Senator Bernie Sanders, during the presidential campaign of 2020. Like all socialists, the Marxists who control higher education like to claim the essentials in life should be free. But they avoid like the plague telling the unescapable truth that nothing is free.

Free college just means American taxpayers—many of whom do not go to college—pick up the tab instead of the students who receive college degrees. This is like asking you to pay for a car you don't own and never get to drive. How much is that tab? The Bernie Sanders plan, borrowed by Joe Biden in 2020, would cost the federal government $47 billion dollars per year. This adds up to more than a trillion dollars over the ten-year period the Sanders plan encompasses. This estimate is low.

Every dime of that obscene amount would come out of your pockets and those of your neighbors. Income tax rates would skyrocket under this plan. The money that supporters of "free" college think they would save would, in reality, come out of their pockets in ever-increasing amounts for the rest of their lives. Of course, this is not a problem in the eyes of Marxists/socialists. In fact, it is precisely what they want. Making Americans dependent on government for education, healthcare, and other essentials is part of their big-picture strategy: gain control of the government, and then, use taxes and regulations to control the people. A dependent populace is a compliant populace. To a Marxist, government is an instrument of control, an instrument—some would say "weapon"—they would wield.

Another problem with the free-college plan proposed by Leftist ideologues is it makes no distinction between legitimate college degrees in high-demand fields and the feel-good identity degrees favored by Marxist college professors and administrators. Require the American taxpayer to pick up the tab for free college and the number of valueless, artificial college degree programs will skyrocket. Further, your taxes will increase just as rapidly as the cost of college tuition has increased over the years. Colleges and universities will lobby Congress continually to increase their federal funding.

Worse yet, in reality college will never be free. While collecting funding for free college tuition from the federal government with one hand, with the other hand educational institutions will continue to charge students for room and board and a long list of ever-increasing fees on top of tuition. Before long, these other sources will cost nearly as much as tuition did before education was "free."

What many American taxpayers don't realize is when it comes to paying for public colleges and universities, they are already picking up approximately 60 percent of the tab, even those who have no children in college. A substantial portion of your state's income tax and sales tax revenues are earmarked for funding community colleges, state colleges, and state universities. Tuition and fees, as high as they are, comprise on average only about 40 percent of a college or university's budget. Your state taxes make up the rest. For this reason and because the political Left wants you to pay 100 percent of the cost of our colleges and universities, you need to be well-informed about this issue.

In a report on the cost of college, the U.S. Bureau of Labor Statistics revealed the average cost of tuition and fees at institutions of higher education in the U.S. increased by 63 percent over a ten-year period from 2006 to 2016. Imagine if your income taxes were to increase by this amount to pay for "free" college tuition. Since the mid-1960s, the average cost of college tuition and fees has increased by 361 percent.[2] Although these increases are extraordinary, they represent only a portion of the total cost of a college education. To the cost of tuition and fees, one must add room and board, books, supplies, and miscellaneous expenses such as transportation, recreation, and entertainment.

If students borrow any or all of the money required to pay for their college education, which many do, the cost of money (interest) must be added to the mix. Finally, one must add an important but hidden cost often overlooked when computing the cost of a college education: the cost of lost income. Students who spend four or more years pursuing a college degree lose the income they would have earned had they worked full-time during those years.

When discussing the actual costs associated with pursuing a college degree, you quickly run into an apples-versus-oranges comparison dilemma. Private universities cost more than public universities, and public universities cost more than community colleges. Further, tuition rates for state-supported institutions vary significantly from state to state with Vermont typically charging the most and Florida the least.[3] What follows is a snapshot of college costs as of this writing. Bear in mind the trend for decades in all of these areas has been for costs to increase rapidly:[4]

- The average cost of tuition at colleges and universities in the U.S. is approximately $36,000 per year, a cost increasing approximately 6.8 percent per year. The upward trend can be expected to continue. For example, after adjusting for inflation the cost of tuition has increased by 361 percent since 1963.
- The cost of books and supplies as of this writing is approximately $1,400 per year and rising. This figure has been held down somewhat by the used book and book rental industries.
- The cost of room and board averages between $10,000 and $12,000 annually depending on whether students live on campus or off. The higher costs are typically for living on campus.
- Miscellaneous expenses including transportation, personal care, and entertainment range from approximately $3,000 to $5,000 annually.
- The cost of lost income—based on just a high school diploma—is approximately $40,000 annually or almost $160,000 over the four years of college. This means a

college graduate who has no student debt begins his or her working life approximately $160,000 in the hole, income that must be made up over the course of a career for the college degree to produce an acceptable return on investment. For students with college-related debt, this number just increases.

• The cost of borrowing money for college depends on the interest rate at the time of the loan. Average student loan debt is approximately $38,000 plus interest compounded every year the individual is in college.

The bottom line you need to understand concerning the financial costs of a college degree is this: for decades, the cost of college tuition has increased more rapidly than all the other goods and services on the Consumer Price Index (CPI) with the exception of healthcare, a trend that continues as of this writing. The financial costs are bad enough, but as was mentioned earlier in this chapter the personal costs associated with pursuing a college degree can be even higher. Four years of Marxist indoctrination can turn your sons and daughters into people you no longer recognize.

THE STUDENT LOAN DEBACLE

One of the worst scams ever perpetrated against the American public is government-backed loans for college students. Federally-backed student loan debt now exceeds $1.5 trillion and is still growing steadily. Because the loans are backed by the federal government, students are able to borrow money recklessly, money many of them have little or no hope of paying back. Further, because the loans are backed by the federal government, banks make loans that violate every principle of responsible lending. But these two problems aren't the worst of it. Four years of Marxist indoctrination turns many college graduates into budding socialists who expect nanny government to "forgive" their loans. This in spite of the fact they know loan "forgiveness" means passing their debts on to others to pay, including many who never got a chance to attend college. Student loans backed by the federal government without any consideration of college major and ability to repay are a bad idea for the very individuals who take out the loans.

Why Student Loans Are a Bad Idea for Individual Borrowers

One of the supposed goals of higher education is to transform college students into contributing, responsible adults who can have a positive effect on their communities and society in general. Allowing young people who are wholly unfamiliar with the concept of borrowing money they must pay back over time with interest can do just the opposite.

As to being contributing citizens, college graduates who chose the wrong major and are buried in student debt have little or nothing left over to contribute. Their lives become an unending marathon of scraping by to make a living while trying to repay a mountainous burden of debt they cannot escape. As to being responsible adults, allowing young people to borrow money to finance college degrees leaving them woefully unprepared to pay the money back is irresponsible lending that encourages irresponsible borrowing.

Few college students look four years down the road and contemplate having to pay back the money they borrow. Like many young people, they live in the moment and worry about the future later. This kind of attitude toward money eventually catches up with them when, after college, they overspend on credit cards and take a casual attitude toward car payments and home mortgages. In addition to encouraging irresponsibility, here are some other reasons federally backed student loans are bad for individual borrowers who choose the wrong college majors:

- Borrowing more than they can pay back and, as a result, failing to make payments on time can have negative consequences that last a lifetime for individual borrowers.
- Not all students who take out student loans complete college. These dropouts are left without a degree of any kind much less a high-demand degree, but they still have to repay the student loan.
- Incurring substantial debt can force individual borrowers into a life that revolves around making monthly payments; one in which they do nothing but work just to keep up. It is not uncommon for heavily indebted college graduates to work full time at one job and part-time at one or more others, thereby reducing the quality of their lives.
- Sporadically missing student loan payments can result in a low credit score preventing individuals from being approved for car loans and home mortgages. It can also result in denial of credit card applications or, at the very least, requirements to pay higher interest rates on credit cards.
- Inability to pay back student loans can lead to insolvency and bankruptcy before the individuals in question even have a chance to get started in life.

The Case against Student Loan "Forgiveness"

Because of the reasons just listed, Congress is lobbied constantly to "forgive" student loans. Much of the lobbying comes from college graduates who finally understand the hole they have dug for themselves. The political pressure to "forgive" students loans is so intense most Leftist congressional and presidential candidates make student loan forgiveness part of their political platforms. This is unfortunate because "forgiving" student loans is a bad idea for numerous reasons including these:

- Calling the concept student loan "forgiveness" is a blatant example of a favorite tactic of Leftist ideologues: *semantic subterfuge*. It amounts to deceptively creating an inoffensive name for an offensive concept. Other examples of semantic subterfuge include calling abortion "choice" and speech control "political correctness." The proper term for this concept is "debt transference." Forgiving student loans means, in reality, transferring the debt from the students who incurred it to taxpayers who did not. Expecting the American taxpayer to pick up the tab for loans for which they had no voice and from which they receive no benefit is unconscionable. There are approximately 250 million adults in America. Of these, approximately 45 million carry student loan debt backed by the federal government. How is it fair to single out these 45 million Americans for special treatment while ignoring the more than 200 million who owe nothing?
- "Forgiving" all federally-backed student loans would add more than $1.5 trillion dollars to America's already out-of-control national debt. Worse yet, if all student debt were to be cancelled today it would re-generate itself within as little time as a year. No student loan "forgiveness" policy yet proposed calls for eliminating federally-backed student loans. Consequently, student loan debt would quickly reconstitute itself and indebted students would expect the same level of "forgiveness" as their predecessors. Worse yet, with an expectation of "forgiveness" established, students would feel free to borrow higher amounts of money, thereby compounding the problem.
- Federally-backed student loans allow colleges and universities to offer meaningless, dumbed-down degree programs because the enrollments are propped up by students borrowing to pay the tuition. If students want

to major in programs with no value in the marketplace, fine; but let them pay their own way through college. There still exists traditional but now rarely used form of financial aid; it's called the J-O-B program. Students get a job and work their way through school. Some of America's most successful, contributing citizens—including the authors—used this program to pay for college. If student loans were available only for students majoring in high-demand programs needed to enhance the competitiveness and security of our country, many of the frivolous degrees now offered would soon dry up and go away and Marxists would have fewer students to indoctrinate.

CHAPTER 6

SECULAR HUMANISM, ATHEISM, AND AGNOSTICISM ON CAMPUS

Religion is anathema to Marxists. As socialists, Marxists put government in the place of God. Consequently, Marxist college professors are secular humanists, atheists, or agnostics; none of which are friendly to Christianity. To briefly distinguish among these three worldviews, secular humanists believe people are able to navigate their way through life applying human logic, reason, and common sense. Therefore, they need no help from a supernatural God. Atheists simply reject the concept of a supernatural God. Agnostics believe the existence of a supernatural God is unknowable, therefore the question of God is mute.

People in each of these categories would give a different answer to the important question, "Do you believe in God?" A secular humanist would respond, "God is not necessary— I can get along fine without him." An atheist would reply, "There is no such thing as God." An agnostic would say, "Who knows and who cares?" What secular humanists, atheists, and agnostics have in common is they all reject the God of Holy Scripture. There is a high likelihood many if not most of the professors your children will be subjected to in college fit into one of these three categories. Those who don't are more likely to be Hindus, Muslims, or Buddhists than Christians.

SECULAR HUMANISM ON CAMPUS

Freedom FROM religion is a fundamental tenet of secular humanism. A secular humanist believes there is no place for the God of Holy Scripture on campus or in any other aspect of public life. The secular humanist interpretation of the First Amendment is it requires a forced segregation of religion from all aspects of public life. This is both a disingenuous and hypocritical interpretation. The disingenuous aspect is secular humanists knowingly and purposefully misinterpret the "Free Exercise" and "Establishment" clauses of the First Amendment.

Here is what these two clauses actual state: "Congress shall make no law respecting an establishment of religion, or prohibiting the free exercise thereof . . ." These words were penned by Christians. We know fifty of the fifty-five framers of the U.S. Constitution were Christians. In addition to ignoring the historical fact that our Founders intended this language to protect citizens against the type of government-mandated, taxpayer-supported national churches found in Europe, their interpretation is disingenuous because it focuses on the first clause and ignores the second. Marxist professors do everything they can to prohibit the free exercise of Christianity on college and university campuses.

What makes the secular humanist interpretation of the First Amendment blatantly hypocritical is they tend to take a hands-off approach to other recognized religions while focusing their repression efforts on Christianity and Judaism. In fact, they typically bend over backward to accommodate Islam, Hinduism, and Buddhism on campus. When it comes to Judaism, they seem to be ambivalent. Perhaps they don't feel threatened by the relatively small number of practicing Jews they encounter in their classes.

Ironically, secular humanists are just as religious as Christians; the difference is found in whom and what they worship. While Christians worship the omniscient, omnipresent God of Holy Scripture, secular humanists worship a limited and ever-changing god—man. But it is not just man universal they worship. Although they are loathe to admit it, secular humanists think they—each individual one of them—is a god. This becomes clear when you examine the most fundamental tenet of the secular-humanist belief system: moral relativism.

Because, as Christians, God is our authority, we believe in right and wrong and look to the Bible for guidance in distinguishing between the two. God's specific revelation concerning who He is, who we are, and how we should live is found in Holy Scripture. Hence, regardless the denomination, the Bible provides a common starting point for helping Christians make determinations about right and wrong. Moral relativism posits there are no absolutes when it comes to right and wrong. Individual secular humanists can decide for themselves what is right and wrong by applying logic, reason, and common sense; never mind human beings tend more toward emotion than logic or reason and common sense is anything but common.

Putting aside for the moment the fact God is the ultimate authority concerning right and wrong, it is important to have a common starting point when discussing and debating such matters. Consider what happens when two people try to settle an issue of right and wrong but lack a common basis for deciding. They are like two surveyors trying to settle a property claim who start their work from two different points of beginning. The claim will never be settled.

The only way one survey can either validate or refute another is if both surveyors started at a common point. The easy-to-grasp lesson in this analogy is one secular humanists—in spite of their supposed superior powers of logic and reason—assiduously ignores. Those who do not wish to be bound by the moral constraints of Christianity must find an alternative. That alternative, at least for many Marxists, is secular humanism. While Christians look to the Bible and the example of Christ for guidance in matters of right and wrong, secular humanists turn to the artificial and easily refuted concept of moral relativism.

Moral Relativism and Secular Humanism

Moral relativism, as was just stated, is a fundamental tenet of the secular humanist's worldview. It claims there are no absolutes when it comes to right and wrong; morality is relative, hence the name. To a secular humanist, right and wrong are culturally based, manmade concepts. This being the case, right and wrong may be determined by individuals.

Secular humanists are fond of claiming, "What's right for you may not be right for me and vice-versa," as if right and wrong are matters of personal taste or preference. When individuals take it upon themselves to determine right and wrong without the guidance of Scripture, they have anointed themselves gods, and human beings are not equipped to be gods. One could drive a truck through the holes in this basic principle of secular humanism. For just one example, moral relativism is self-refuting. To state there are no absolutes is to state an absolute.

Secular humanists believe in the evolutionary view that life on earth is the result of countless cosmic accidents. This being the case, life is random and, therefore, lacks any meaning more substantive than whatever makes an individual happy at the moment. Consequently, anything that makes you happy in the moment is acceptable because in the long run it is not going to matter anyway. From the convenient perspective of moral relativism, if something is right for me, it is right period—a seductive point of view for those who don't want to be constrained by Judeo-Christian ethics. Moral relativism allows people to live sinful lives without having to admit they are doing so. In adopting moral relativism as part of their worldview, secular humanists are applying a strategy as old as mankind itself: if the rules get in the way of what you want, change the rules.

Is Moral Relativism Morally Neutral?

Secular humanists like to claim moral relativism is morally neutral. This, of course, is a practical impossibility; nothing is morally neutral. By moral neutrality, secular humanists mean they are completely impartial, make no judgments, and tolerate all opinions when it comes to deciding right and wrong or when confronted with the opinions, ideas, or beliefs of others. Really? Are Marxist professors being morally neutral when they demand conformance to their secular humanist and socialist worldviews while belittling Christianity?

When secular humanists argue for moral relativism, they argue against themselves. For example, tell a proponent of moral relativism you advocate child abuse and you are likely to be reported to government authorities. However, if the secular humanist who reports you really believes right and wrong are matters of individual choice, how can he or she argue against child abuse? After all, there are certainly individuals—many of them—who choose to abuse children.

Because of this inherent flaw in their philosophy, secular humanists have taken to adding a disclaimer to their arguments for moral relativism. They now claim whatever the individual believes is right unless it hurts someone else. But, of course, the disclaimer is as flawed as the concept. If everything is relative, it cannot be wrong to hurt someone else. If it is wrong to hurt someone else, why then do Marxist professors who worship at the altar of moral relativism participate in denying tenure to or even firing Christian and conservative professors? Why do they belittle, attack, and discriminate against Christian students?

By their own professed definition, these harmful actions are wrong. After all, they certainly hurt the Christian and conservative professors and students who are the victims. How do moral relativists justify supporting abortion when the child whose life is taken is certainly hurt, as is the mother, whether she realizes it or not—not to mention society in general? There is no end to these kinds of questions, nor is there an acceptable answer to them from proponents of moral relativism. Secular humanists who claim logic is one of their most fundamental assets somehow lose all logic when it comes to defending their beliefs.

Obviously, moral relativism is a flawed concept. Nonetheless, it is considered sacred ground among Marxist professors. Yet, these same professors are quick to claim Christian and conservative worldviews are wrong, or even worse. Where is the tolerance that is supposed to accompany their "morally-neutral" views? Once again, one could drive a truck through the holes in moral relativism. Like any concept based on the god of man instead of the God of Holy Scripture, it quickly falls apart in practice.

Humanist Manifesto: The Bible for Secular Humanists/Moral Relativists

Although its proponents refuse to admit it, secular humanism is a religion. It has a god—the individual—and a "bible"—the *Humanist Manifesto*. There are actually three versions of the Manifesto: *Humanist Manifesto I* published in 1933, *Humanist Manifesto II* published in 1973, and *Humanism and Its Aspirations* published in 2003 (Humanist Manifesto III). All three of these books describe a worldview devoid of the God of Holy Scripture or any other kind of higher power. All three versions of the Manifesto have been signed by prominent Leftist ideologues and Marxist professors, but not without some controversy.

The Manifesto has been updated and revised over time as humanist thinking has ebbed and flowed and as disagreements among proponents of secular humanism have emerged as a result; the fickle nature of man being just one of many factors undermining the fundamental validity of a man-centered religion. Consequently, each successive version of the Manifesto has sought to correct the perceived weaknesses of its predecessor and settle controversies among secular humanists.

Humanist Manifesto I. The original Manifesto was written in 1933. It presented a new belief system to replace religions founded on supernatural revelation. The new belief system it proposed amounted to an egalitarian worldview based on voluntary mutual cooperation among all people; an ideal rendered impossible from the outset by the sinful nature of man. Predictably, there were disagreements about various aspects of the Manifesto among those involved in developing it, a circumstance inherent in all human endeavors. Consequently, the originally proposed title, *The Humanist Manifesto*, had to be changed to *A Humanist Manifesto*.

Ironically, the original Manifesto contained a basic tenet that now haunts, embarrasses, and even angers modern-day secular humanists. It referred to humanism as a religion; something its proponents now go to great lengths to deny since freedom *from* religion is the cornerstone of their man-centered worldview. If secular humanists admit their views of morality are a religion, the hypocrisy of their efforts to ban religion from the classroom, public square, and every other aspect of everyday life is exposed. When this happens, secular humanists find it difficult to deny Christianity is their real target, not religion—something even a casual observer of the American culture wars already knows.

Humanist Manifesto II. The horrors of World War II perpetrated by Hitler, Stalin, and Tojo, exploded the ideal at the heart of the original Manifesto. With the evidence of Hitler's death camps, Stalin's pogroms, and Tojo's rape of Nanking revealed to the world, even the most idealistic humanists had to admit their hope for a worldwide egalitarian society based on voluntary mutual cooperation might have been overly optimistic, not to mention naive. One can only wonder why the horrors of World War II did not lead humanists to abandon their principle of moral relativism.

Admitting the naivety of the first document, drafters of the revised Manifesto took a more realistic approach. Rather than pursuing a worldwide egalitarian society based on voluntary mutual cooperation, the drafters of *Manifesto II* set more "realistic" goals including the elimination of war and poverty.

None of the document's authors or supporters thought to ask how these goals could be achieved without changing the heart of man. This is how it is and has always been with secular humanists. Since individuals are gods, why try to change their hearts? When one will not admit man has a sinful nature, it is easy to naively think war and hunger can be eliminated by simply displaying heart-tugging bumper stickers on your car. After all, surely such slogans as "Give Peace a Chance"—if displayed on enough bumpers—will end war.

One of the most controversial and frequently quoted verses from *Manifesto II* is: "Humans are responsible for what we are and what we will become. No deity will save us; we must save ourselves."[1] It should come as no surprise to find this kind of language in a document published by the American Humanist Association, an organization with the motto

"Good Without a God" and a purpose statement which reads "Advocating Progressive Values and Equality for Humanists, Atheists, and Freethinkers."[2]

Another verse from Manifesto II, one clearly revealing a cherished goal of secular humanists is:

> I am convinced the battleground for humankind's future must be waged and won in the public school classroom by teachers who correctly perceive their role as the proselytizers of a new faith: a religion of humanity that recognizes and respects the spark of what theologians call divinity in every human being. . . . utilizing a classroom instead of a pulpit to convey humanist values in whatever subject they teach, regardless of the educational level—preschool day care or large state university.[3]

As is always the case in the endeavors of man, there was much disagreement in the humanist community about various aspects of Manifesto II. Consequently, only a few ardent proponents agreed to sign the document when it was first released. To solve this problem, the Manifesto has since been widely circulated with a caveat making it clear it is not necessary to agree with every detail of the document in order to be a signatory. This disclaimer had the intended effect and the document eventually garnered more signatures. This is like claiming you do not have to accept the whole Bible to be a Christian; you can pick and choose the parts of Scripture you agree with. That has certainly not worked well for the American church.

Humanist Manifesto III. The latest version of the Manifesto—Humanist Manifesto III—is titled, *Humanism and Its Aspirations*. It was published by the American Humanist Association in 2003. This version of the Manifesto is purposefully shorter than its predecessors. It presents six broad beliefs encompassing the humanist philosophy as professed by the American Humanist Association while leaving plenty of wiggle room for different interpretations. Leaving room for different interpretations was necessary to avoid the level of disagreement within humanist circles surrounding the two early versions of the Manifesto. These six broad statements of belief may be summarized as follows:[4]

1. Knowledge of the world is empirically derived (by observation, experimentation, and rational analysis).
2. Unguided evolutionary change has the result of making humans integral to nature.
3. Ethical values are established by humans and are based on human need that has been tested by experience.
4. Humans are fulfilled in life by participating in the service of humane ideals.
5. Humans are, by nature, social beings. Therefore, they find meaning in relationships.
6. Humans maximize their happiness by working to benefit society.

Although these six statements of belief are not as specific as those contained in the early versions, they still support the same worldview. For example, the first statement—the humanist belief in empiricism—rules out God's special revelation as set forth in the Bible and reveals an astounding ignorance of the philosophical problems inherent in man-centered empiricism. The second statement is a reiteration of the humanist belief in Darwinian evolution which, of course, is the American Humanist Association's justification for supporting abortion.

The third statement makes clear the Bible has no place in establishing right and wrong. Rather, what is right or wrong depends on human need. The last three statements make clear the humanist's rejection of God, the Bible, and religion. In the fourth statement, fulfillment comes from the service of humane ideals, not service to God and His Kingdom. Christians also believe in service, but they know service to man comes from Christ's admonition to love your neighbor as yourself.

In the fifth statement, human relationships are presented as the ultimate goal, as opposed to a relationship with God. Finally, humanists believe service to society is the ultimate service because, for them, man is God. Christians also believe in service to society, but as a way to serve the God who created man and to follow Christ's admonition to love our neighbors as ourselves.

Manifesto III is shorter and more to the point than its predecessors, and its six statements of belief are less specific, but its rejection of God is just as much a cornerstone as it was in the early versions. The wording and length of the various versions of the manifesto have changed over time, but its foundational man-as-god philosophy has not. Herein is found the never-changing source of the unbridgeable gulf between secular humanism and Christianity. Herein also is found the source of the religious bigotry toward Christianity, the core characteristic of secular humanism.

Secular humanists apparently believe they can peacefully co-exist with other religions—hence their accommodation on campus of Islam, Hinduism, and Buddhism—but not with Christianity. Although there is a philosophical train wreck coming farther down the track involving secular humanists and Islam, for now they have focused their animosity on Christianity because they know if Christianity is right, they are wrong. This simple fact frightens Marxist faculties dominated by secular humanists so much they feel compelled to belittle, attack, and even suppress the Christian worldview in every way possible on campus.

Secular Humanist's Rationale for Moral Relativism

Because their god is the individual, it was necessary for secular humanists to establish an ethical corollary to humanism that would render absolute standards of right and wrong obsolete. "During much of early American history, moral education in colleges and universities moved from being grounded in appeals to special revelation [the Bible] to universal appeals to human nature, natural law, or reason."[5]

Thus, moral relativism is an artificial concept manufactured by secular humanists to replace God with man. A fundamental flaw in the concept its proponents have never been able to adequately explain is the only things common to all humanity are its creation by God and its sinful nature, neither of which secular humanists can admit to. One of the least common characteristics of man is reason. Nevertheless, when individuals are gods with all of their inherent moral frailties, moral relativism is the best secular humanists could do in trying to establish a workable ethical framework.

In order for secular humanism to prevail in American society, it is necessary for its proponents to control or at least influence the institutions that, together, weave the tapestry of our moral, cultural, and social conventions. This is why secular humanists are so intent on dominating education at all levels. The institutions with the greatest impact on shaping our moral, cultural, and social conventions are the family, church, and education.

Since Secular humanists cannot dominate the family and church—although they are making progress in both areas—they chose to focus on gaining control of education at all levels. They understood in doing so he who controls education in America controls America's future. To control education, it was necessary to sever its Christian roots. This is why secular humanists need to suppress the moral absolutes of Christianity and replace them with the ever-changing whims of moral relativism.

Values Neutrality and Christianity in Higher Education?

One of the arguments advanced by moral relativists to justify suppressing biblical views on campus is higher education should be values neutral. This argument is not only specious, it's laughable, an argument made to appeal to the naïve. Those who make this argument claim values should be addressed by the family and church rather than institutions of higher education.

Christians certainly agree families and churches should play the key role in establishing values in society. However, there are several problems with this argument, the most fundamental of them being it represents a practical impossibility. Even if Marxist professors tried to be values neutral, they could not possibly achieve such a goal. There is no such thing as a values neutral individual. Another problem with this argument is the hypocrisy in it. Marxist professors go out of their way to undermine the values they claim should be left to the development of families and churches. They are hardly neutral when it comes to Christian and conservative values.

On this subject, Anne Colby wrote: ". . . closer scrutiny makes it clear that educational institutions cannot be values neutral. For decades educators have recognized the power of the 'hidden curriculum' in schools and the moral messages it carries. The hidden curriculum is the (largely unexamined) practices through which the school and its teachers operate, maintaining discipline, assigning grades and other rewards, and managing their relationships with their students and each other."[6]

Marxist professors know families and the church help young people develop a moral compass that determines how they interpret the input they receive as well as how they perceive the world. This is why they are so determined to supplant the Christian worldview with one embracing moral relativism. Marxist professors who assign lower grades to students whose work reflects their Christian beliefs and who are adversarial in their relationships with Christian and conservative students are hardly values neutral. Further, they don't want their students to be values neutral. They want students to forget the values they learned in the home and church and embrace secular humanism, moral relativism, and Marxism.

Moral Relativism Poses a Dilemma for Marxist Professors and Institutions

Secular humanists, with their devotion to moral relativism, are continually sticking their heads in an intellectual vise. One jaw of the vise is their professed beliefs, and the other is the consequences of those beliefs. Marxist faculties cling tenaciously to the non-absolutes of moral relativism while, at the same time, deploring their consequences—consequences such as cheating, sloppy work, mushy-headed thinking, and irresponsible behavior on the part of students.

If morality is relative and self-determined, then cheating is wrong only if one gets caught because honesty has value only to the extent it serves one's purpose at the moment. If morality is relative, then an individual's only responsibility is to his or her own personal needs at any given point in time. Further, it is apparent that students—no matter what their worldviews may be—do not learn to respect each other, their professors, or the teaching-learning process by seeing their Christian and conservative peers being treated disrespectfully.

When there is only one point of view allowed in a discussion, is it any wonder students fail to develop critical thinking skills and become mushy-headed in their reasoning?

When students are taught what to think rather than how to think, is it any wonder they have to be spoon-fed dumbed-down material? These are the kinds of conundrums Marxist faculties inflict on themselves by advocating moral relativism while suppressing Christian and conservative views.

That universities suffering the consequences of their advocacy of moral relativism should surprise no one, except perhaps Marxist professors who are blinded by their own self-serving ideology. Few issues better illustrate the bind institutions of higher education put themselves in by embracing moral relativism than rampant cheating.

Rampant Cheating on Campus: A Consequence of Moral Relativism

Archie and David (two of your authors) spent almost eighty years in education holding positions including instructor, professor, department chair, division director, librarian, dean, provost, and vice-president. This experience allows us to state without hesitation the goal of a lot of college students is receiving a degree, not an education.

Couple this outlook on education with a morally relativistic view of honesty and enable students with advanced technologies and you have the perfect storm for epidemic cheating by college students. Term papers downloaded from the internet, tests stolen electronically using the photographic function of cell phones, and test answers text-messaged to friends during tests are just a few of the technology-enhanced approaches to cheating in college. There are many more.

Student cheating has become so endemic on college and university campuses that protecting against it has become a growth industry. There are seminars to teach faculty members how to spot cheating in their classes, software to detect plagiarism, test banks allowing teachers to give every student a different set of test questions, and countless other tools to combat cheating. While cheating is good for the rapidly growing anti-cheating industry, it is undermining the integrity of higher education.

Marxist institutions are equipped to do little more than treat the symptoms. To get at the cause would require them to re-think their allegiance to moral relativism. Meanwhile the principles of moral relativism so deeply ingrained in our nation's universities do not remain on campus. Every graduating class from every college and university in America is filled with new recruits to moral relativism who, seeing no problem with it, cheat in all areas of their lives. Their moral relativism then shows up in a variety of different forms of corruption infecting society.

The Case against Moral Relativism

Perhaps the most appealing aspect of moral relativism to a secular humanist is it allows them to get away with doing whatever they want. It is the perfect philosophical construct for people who do not wish to have their behavior constrained or their lifestyle inhibited by the rules. This aspect of moral relativism is why Ryan Dobson calls the concept "sin in a toga," by which he means it is little more than "selfishness and hedonism and rebellion dressed up in philosopher's robes."[7]

In his book *Be Intolerant: Because Some Things Are Just Stupid*, Dobson says:

> Moral relativism is not a philosophy you would arrive at by studying the world around you. If you put something under your microscope or do real science with your chemistry set or point your telescope at the stars, you will not arrive at the conclusion that there are no constants in the universe. The only way to come up with moral relativism is

to begin with an agenda and then look for ways to
make your agenda possible. Your starting point is
not an observation of the universe, but an action
you want to take.[8]

This is an important point because one of the foundational
tenets of secular humanism is empiricism: knowledge of the
world is gained through observation, experimentation, and
rational analysis as opposed to biblical revelation. Empiricism actually refutes moral relativism. Dobson explains why
the easily refuted concept of moral relativism is what he calls
a "broken philosophy:"[9] Moral relativism is empty, meaningless, and purposeless. It can provide permission to do what
should not be done or to tolerate what should not be toler-
ated, but it cannot provide hope. Nor can it give its proponents peace or answers to life's quandaries, problems,
or mysteries.

   According to Dobson, moral relativism is self-refuting.
The idea there is no absolute truth—the cornerstone of
moral relativism—is itself a declaration of absolute truth.
People cling to moral relativism in the same way and for the
same reason smokers continue to smoke: they want what it
does for them more than they want the benefits of quit-
ting.[10] Secular humanists claim to worship logic, reason, and
common sense, but their allegiance to moral relativism lacks
all three.

ATHEISM AND AGNOSTICISM ON CAMPUS

Not all Marxist professors are secular humanists; some are
atheists and some are agnostics. As was mentioned at the
beginning of this chapter, there are distinctions among these
three philosophies, but the distinctions are just matters of
degree. All three reject Christianity. Whereas secular
humanists believe man can do just fine without God, atheists

reject the very idea of God. Agnostics think the concept of God is irrelevant because it cannot be verified. To an agnostic, maybe there is a God and maybe not. Secular humanism is a much broader concept than atheism or agnosticism. Whereas secular humanism qualifies as a religion, atheism and agnosticism do not. What the three have in common is they are man-centered philosophies lacking the direction of a supreme being.

Of the three philosophies, the majority of Marxist professors subscribe to secular humanism and atheism. Few are agnostics. This means there is a high probability Christian and conservative college students will spend four or more years under the tutelage of professors who reject God. In spite of such supposedly sacrosanct principles as academic freedom and freedom of speech, a lot of these professors approach students from a coercive perspective, "You have to buy what I am selling or you won't pass."

To illustrate how far Marxist institutions will go to drive God out of the classroom, off the campus, and out of the lives of students, consider this ironic fact: in 2021, Harvard University chose an atheist as its new chief chaplain. You read that right—an atheist chaplain. If "atheist chaplain" strikes you as an oxymoron, it should. Harvard's chief chaplain, Greg Epstein, an atheist, is the author of the book *Good Without God: What a Billion Nonreligious People Do Believe.*[11] In his defense, Epstein was elected by his fellow university chaplains, although this just suggests religion—particularly Christianity—is a low priority at Harvard.

Epstein believes people can be good human beings and lead ethical lives without God. But this belief raises several important questions. What is a good human being? Who decides what it means to be a good human being? Is it something people vote on? How do you resolve differences in meaning? As for leading ethical lives, this means leading lives that accord with a set of moral principles. Where do those principles come from—what is their source? How are disagreements about morality resolved?

Is Epstein willing to take up the cause of Christian students at Harvard whose views are belittled and suppressed by Marxist professors? How does an atheist professor deal with students whose problems are caused by their own impatience, pride, covetousness, envy, hatred, and malice? A Christian chaplain could open the Bible and show students where these kinds of behaviors are proscribed. He could then turn to Galatians 5:22–23 where the fruit of the Spirit is shown to consist of love, joy, peace, patience, kindness, goodness, faithfulness, gentleness, and self-control. What source does an atheist chaplain turn to?

Whether the professors Christian children study under in college are secular humanists, atheists, or agnostics, they represent a clear and present danger to students whose belief system is grounded in Holy Scripture. As a result, a lot of Christian families send their children away for a college education only to find they have been indoctrinated instead and returned home as Marxist minions who hate God and hate America.

CHAPTER 7

THE LEFT'S WAR ON GOD, COUNTRY, AND CONSERVATIVES

The examples of Marxist tyranny presented throughout this book are not just isolated cases perpetrated by rogue elements of the Left who have strayed from the norm. Rather, they are small skirmishes in a much larger war being conducted against God, country, and Conservatives—particularly on university campuses. The tactics employed by the Left in conducting this war violate the principles of free speech, free thought, and free inquiry academic freedom was established to protect.

In an article entitled "Diversity Dishonesty on College Campuses," Phyllis Schlafly wrote:

> Diversity, multiculturalism, tolerance, and political correctness are the watchwords in colleges and universities today. The campus thought police have defined those words to enforce the liberal leftwing agenda. Diversity means diversity only for thoughts and practices that are politically correct. Political correctness means conformity to leftwing orthodoxy. Multiculturalism means all

cultures are equal but Western Judeo-Christian civilization is the worst. Tolerance means acceptance of all behaviors except those that comport with the Ten Commandments.[1]

David Horowitz comments on the tactics employed by the Left in conducting its war on God, country, and Conservatives in an article titled, "The Surreal World of the Progressive Left." Horowitz writes:

> It is not for nothing that George Orwell had to invent terms like "double-think" and "double-speak" to describe the universe totalitarians created. Those who have watched the left as long as I have, understand the impossible task that progressives confront in conducting their crusades. Rhetorically, they are passionate proponents of "equality" but in practice they are committed enthusiasts of a hierarchy of privilege in which the highest ranks are reserved for themselves as the guardians of righteousness, than for those they designate "victims" and "oppressed," who are thus worthy of their redemption. Rhetorically they are secularists and avatars of tolerance, but in fact they are religious fanatics who regard their opponents as sinners and miscreants and agents of civil darkness. Therefore, when they engage an opponent, it is rarely to examine and refute his argument but rather to destroy the bearer of the argument and remove him from the plain of battle.[2]

One of the most effective weapons in the arsenal of the radical Left is the American Civil Liberties Union (ACLU), an organization instrumental in helping Marxists conduct their war on God, country, and Conservatives. This is what the Alliance Defending Freedom says about the ACLU and its efforts in this war:

> For more than 50 years, the ACLU and other radical activist groups have attempted to eliminate public expression of our nation's faith and heritage. They have done this through fear, intimidation, misinformation, and filing of lawsuits (or threats of lawsuits) that would: eliminate Christian and historic faith symbols from government documents, buildings, and monuments; ban public prayer in schools and at school functions; deny Christians the right to use public facilities that are open to other groups, and prevent Christians from expressing their faith in the workplace.[3]

HOW MARXISTS VIEW CHRISTIANS AND CONSERVATIVES

It is difficult for those outside the academy to understand how virulent the Left's attacks on God, country, and Conservatives can be or how deeply felt is their animosity. People often have a distorted or, at least, ill-informed view of life in higher education. They tend to view the academy as a place where diverse points of view are welcomed, and where bright people debate their differing views in a supportive and collegial environment. In other words, they think the scholarly environment in higher education is what it should be. When people who hold these misinformed views are provided examples to the contrary, they are shocked to have the myth shattered.

Consequently, in this section we provide examples of how the Left views Christians and Conservatives, quoting their own words to make our point. For example, Peter Singer, a bioethics professor from Princeton University said this about God: "If we don't play God, who will? There seems to me to be three possibilities: there is a God, but He doesn't care about evil and suffering; there is a God who cares, but He or She is a bit of an underachiever; or there is no God. Personally, I believe the latter."[4]

Such sentiments are not limited to faculty members at the Ivy League institutions. Professor Steven Weinberg of the University of Texas had this to say about religion: "I think in many respects religion is a dream—a beautiful dream often. . . . But it's a dream from which I think it's about time we awoke. Just as a child learns about the tooth fairy and is incited by that to leave a tooth under the pillow—and you are glad the child believes in the tooth fairy. But eventually you want the child to grow up."[5]

Writing about Christians, John Indo suggested they be required to take a class in logic, but then opined it would probably do no good because: ". . . then we would face another problem in making them respond to it. Logical thinking is antithetical to the far religious right—except, of course, when it is used to propound their strictly ad hoc arguments. . . . Their limited little minds function only in support of parochialist stupidity. . . . We must stop them at all costs."[6]

Indo summarizes accurately and concisely the agenda of the radical Left. It is not sufficient to just ridicule, persecute, and intimidate Christians and Conservatives—they must be stopped. As should be clear from these few quotes, the radical Left is making war on God, country, and Conservatives, and they intend to win.

THE RADICAL LEFT'S ATTACKS ON CAMPUS FREEDOMS

Reporting is replete with examples of attacks on campus freedoms by soldiers of the radical Left. To get a feel for how widespread and frequent these attacks are, consider the following representative cases:[7]

- The State University of New York at Buffalo (SUNY Buffalo) established a speech code that on the surface appeared to do little more than encourage good manners, but the code is a wolf in sheep's clothing. The code made any speech in residence halls that is not courteous, polite, or mannerly impermissible. While universities may certainly establish codes of conduct to protect students' ability to sleep and study in dormitories, restricting all speech in a dormitory to that which is courteous, polite, and mannerly is just one more way of silencing the views of students and their ability to voice them. Who decides what is courteous and polite? With such a speech code in place, any student who happens to voice disagreement with another student's lifestyle, behavior, or personal choices could be charged and disciplined. Since Christian students are going to see plenty of behavior in university dormitories they disagree with, they are likely to be the most frequent targets of speech code violations.

- A Christian was arrested and charged with trespassing after sharing his faith on the campus of Schenectady County Community College. The student was speaking about his faith and distributing religious tracts in a public area of the campus, when the college's assistant dean told him to stop preaching and leave the campus or be arrested, a clear violation of Davis's First Amendment rights.

- Officials at Shippensburg University used provisions in the institution's speech code to strip a Christian student organization of its rights and privileges because it required members to honor a statement of faith and because it selected its leaders according to its interpretation of biblical teaching.

- Two students at Georgia Institute of Technology were subjected to religious discrimination for maintaining a biblical view of homosexuality, a view violating the university's "Safe Space" training program. The "Safe Space" program ridiculed religions that did not embrace homosexuality.
- A Christian speaker at Southeastern Louisiana University was told he had to have a permit in order to share his faith. When he tried to engage others in conversation about their faith at a location on campus designated for outside speakers, campus police intervened and informed him he needed a permit. University officials then informed the student his application for a permit had to be filed seven days in advance. If approved, he would be restricted to a two-hour block of time every seven days. In order to apply, he would be required to pay a fee, divulge his Social Security number, and submit information about the content of his speech.
- Temple University censored the religious and conservative views of a student who was a member of the Pennsylvania National Guard claiming his views violated the school's speech code. He was prohibited from making religious and conservative statements in class and in conversations with other students.
- The University of Maryland-Baltimore County inhibited a pro-life group's efforts to share its message on campus. A student reserved space for the Rock of Life Club's "Genocide Awareness Project" and permission was granted. Originally approved for display in front of the University Center, permission was quickly rescinded by university officials, who required the club to move the display to a succession of different locations, each more isolated than the previous location. The final location was a vacant lot far removed from student traffic.

These examples are representative of what is taking place on college and university campuses nationwide. The radical Left is persistent and increasingly aggressive in its attempts to silence Christian and conservative speech, thought, and inquiry. On the other hand, Christians and Conservatives are fighting back using the strategies and tactics explained later in this book. For example, most of the cases cited above were successfully resolved in favor of Christians and Conservative students through legal action by the Alliance Defending Freedom.

ATTACKING AMERICA BY REVISING ITS HISTORY

If you wish to undermine a country, undermine its institutions and its history. This is precisely what the radical Left is doing in America, and with evident success. The Left has made great strides in undermining the family, polluting the public school system, and dominating colleges and universities. But some of its most nefariously effective work has been in revising America's history.

In his book *The Death of the West*, Patrick Buchanan explains how in 1992, UCLA received a two-million-dollar grant from the National Endowment for the Humanities and the U.S. Department of Education to develop new standard for history books for grades five through twelve. UCLA completed this assignment in 1997. Its standards have had the intended effect. According to Buchanan, UCLA's standards for history books for public school children have resulted in the following:[8]

- There is no mention in history books of such American luminaries as Samuel Adams, Paul Revere, Thomas Edison, Alexander Graham Bell, or the Wright Brothers.
- The founding dates of the Sierra Club and the National Organization for Women are given special significance.

- Instructions for teachers concerning how to teach the unit which covers the traitor Alger Hiss and the spies Ethel and Julius Rosenberg encourages leeway to teach the unit as if Hiss was not a traitor and the Rosenbergs were innocent. (The Rosenbergs gave America's atombomb secrets to Joseph Stalin and were convicted by a jury of their peers.)
- The Constitutional Convention is not even mentioned.
- George Washington's presidency is not mentioned nor is his famous farewell address. Rather than learn about the two terms of our country's first president, students are encouraged to develop an imaginary dialogue between an Indian leader and General Washington at the end of the Revolutionary War.
- The Soviet Union is commended for its great strides in space exploration, but America's moon landing is not mentioned.
- Teachers are urged to have students conduct a mock trial for John D. Rockefeller of Standard Oil.
- Students are encouraged to study the skills and architecture of the Aztecs, but there is no mention of their practice of human sacrifice.

The new history standards developed by UCLA have had far-reaching effects. Look at any history book written for public school students and you will be appalled at what is included and what is not. There are now history books giving more coverage to Madonna than to George Washington. Further, America is often portrayed as a villainous nation bent on world dominance, imperialism, the perpetuation of slavery, and a variety of other evils.

One widely used history book devotes just one page to World War II. In that one page, the authors write only about the atomic bombs dropped on Hiroshima and Nagasaki. They portray the United States as an evil empire for dropping the bombs. Hypocritically, there is no mention of such Japanese atrocities as the sneak attack on Pearl Harbor, the brutal Bataan death march, the rape of Nanking, or the extraordinarily high death rate of American POWs.

What you won't find in any of the textbooks written according to the UCLA guidelines is positive coverage of the U.S. Constitution, a document guaranteeing the rights of Leftist ideologues to attack and undermine America. You will find no mention of the fact the Constitution protects these hypocrites even as they do their best to destroy our country.

HOW THE LEFT SINGLES OUT CHRISTIANS IN HIGHER EDUCATION

When the radical Left is allowed to undermine America's families, public schools, universities, military, and history, we all suffer, at least indirectly. But there are Christians and Conservatives, especially in higher education, who suffer directly for their beliefs. This section chronicles the trials and tribulations of a representative few eminently qualified professors who, because of their religious and scientific beliefs, have been attacked by the radical Left.

Professor Emeritus Richard H. Bube of Stanford University

Dr. Bube led a seminar titled *Issues in Science and Religion* for more than twenty-five years at Stanford University. It was well received by students. However, when Stanford's administration became concerned about Bube holding Christian views and making them known to students, the popular seminar was cancelled without notice or explanation. Fortunately for Stanford's students, Bube was not a man easily put off. Further, the Left's favorite tactic of claiming those who espouse a Christian worldview are not scientists could not be easily applied to Dr. Bube.

Bube holds a Bachelor of Science Degree in physics from Brown University and a PhD in physics from Princeton. He served as a member of the research staff at the RCA David Sarnoff Research Laboratories at Princeton from 1948 to 1962. He also served as section head for the photo-electronic materials group. He joined the faculty at Stanford in 1962 and became chairman of the Department of Materials Science. In 1992, Bube became emeritus professor of materials science at Stanford in recognition of his forty-four years of distinguished service in the field. An internationally known scientist, Bube is also a widely recognized expert on the intersections between science and religion. He is a prodigious writer on both science and the interaction of science and religion.[9]

The popularity of Bube's seminar coupled with his status in the scientific community presented Stanford's dominant anti-Christianity elite with a difficult problem: how to silence Bube's Christian views without creating a backlash from students, scientists, and Christians. What they did not anticipate—and should have—were the intellect and determination of Dr. Bube. Intellectually speaking, the contest was one of gnats pestering a giant.

Stanford formed a committee to handle the situation. Unable to provide the real reason for cancelling the seminar, the committee attempted to engage in scholarly subterfuge, throwing a smokescreen of doublespeak about the seminar and trying to use a favorite academic tactic: paralysis by analysis. Bube was not taken in nor was he deterred by the committee's stalling and subterfuge. He calmly answered all of their concerns, challenged their unfounded accusations, and refuted their false claims. When doublespeak and paralysis by analysis did not work, the committee upped the ante and switched to intimidation and harassment.

The committee wanted Bube to agree to teach the seminar from an orthodox Darwinian point of view. Like most members of the radical Left, they harbored a deep fear that even a moderately friendly treatment of theistic evolution or intelligent design—not to mention creationism—by a distinguished scholar and scientist such a Dr. Bube might change the thinking of those they worked so hard to indoctrinate. It took patience, persistence, and a towering intellect, but eventually Bube was able to pin down the committee concerning their real agenda. After two years of academic jousting with the committee, Bube was once again allowed to teach his seminar—a better result than most Christian professors enjoy.[10]

Professor Emeritus Dean Kenyon of San Francisco State University

Dr. Kenyon was a committed evolutionist for most of his career and as such won the respect of his colleagues in the Marxist scientific community. However, through research into the ability of chemicals to become naturally arranged into complex information-bearing molecules, Kenyon began to doubt the Darwinian explanation. Finally, after much research and study he concluded his Darwinian views were flawed and he could no longer accept them. Dr. Kenyon began to discuss the evidence against Darwinian evolution in his classes at San Francisco State.

Kenyon's department chair gave him a direct order not to discuss creationism in his class. It is interesting to note how Leftist ideologues who are so opposed to the military can be so quick to adopt the military approach of giving direct orders when there is a threat to their Darwinian orthodoxy. Then the department chair made it clear only non-theistic evolution could be taught at San Francisco State University. Finally, Kenyon was removed from the classroom and assigned primarily to teaching and monitoring labs, an assignment typically given to graduate assistants.[11]

To get a feel for just how vicious a tactic this was, compare and contrast Kenyon's credentials with those of the graduate students who in essence became his new colleagues as lab instructors. Graduate students are just that—students. They are working toward either a master's or doctorate degree, a goal they may or may not achieve. Kenyon, on the other hand, is a highly qualified, well-respected scientist with numerous publication credits. He holds a bachelor's degree in physics from the University of Chicago and a PhD in physics from Stanford. He has been a National Science Foundation Postdoctoral Fellow at the University of California at Berkeley, a visiting scholar at Oxford University, and a Postdoctoral fellow at the National Aeronautics and Space Administration (NASA) Ames Research Center. Kenyon is the coauthor of one of the two best-selling advanced-level books on the subject of chemical evolution.[12]

To reduce a scholar of Kenyon's reputation, stature, and credentials to teaching lab classes is a travesty and a waste, and all because he had the audacity to question the validity of Darwinian evolution. For baseball fans, this sad case is akin to reducing homerun king and Hall of Famer, Hank Aaron, to the position of batboy during his prime, and for football fans it is like demoting NFL stars Tom Brady or Peyton Manning to ball boys.

Professor Guillermo Gonzalez of Iowa State University

One of the most telling cases in the radical Left's persecution of those who fail to toe the line of Marxist orthodoxy is that of Professor Guillermo Gonzalez of Iowa State University. Gonzalez was born in Cuba, but his family fled to the United States in 1967, where he went on to earn a PhD in astronomy from the University of Washington. An accomplished scientist, Dr. Gonzalez has published almost seventy peer-reviewed scientific papers and is the coauthor of a major college-level textbook on astronomy. His research led to the discovery of two new planets and his work has been featured in *Science*, *Nature*, and *Scientific American*.[13]

In 2004, Dr. Gonzalez coauthored a book titled *The Privileged Planet: How Our Place in the Cosmos Is Designed for Discovery*. This book presents empirical evidence in support of intelligent design. It was shortly after the publication of this book when Gonzalez's problems began. According to the Discovery Institute, when the book was released, a religious studies professor who was the faculty advisor to the campus Atheist and Agnostic Society began a campaign against Gonzalez. As a result, Dr. Gonzalez was denied tenure.[14] Denial of tenure is the academic equivalent of the death sentence. Once tenure is permanently denied, the faculty member in question is typically terminated.

The tenure process at ISU appears to have been not just controlled but manipulated by a group of Gonzalez's colleagues determined to silence his views on intelligent design. According to ISU's Department of Physics and Astronomy, to earn a promotion from assistant professor to associate professor (gain tenure), a faculty member must meet the following requirement: ". . . excellence sufficient to lead to a national or international reputation is required and would ordinarily be shown by the publication of approximately fifteen papers of good quality in refereed journals."[15] Since Dr. Gonzalez published sixty-eight refereed scientific papers at the time of his tenure hearing, he should have easily made the grade. In fact, his record of scholarly publications was better than all but one of the members of his tenure committee.

After reviewing the case, the Discovery Institute claims, "Documents show Gonzalez was denied fair tenure process by hostile colleagues who plotted behind his back, suppressed evidence, and then misled the public."[16] The Institute provides the following information, which it learned by examining documents relating to the Gonzalez tenure process and decision obtained under the Iowa Open Records Act:[17]

- Dr. Gonzalez was subjected to a covert campaign of innuendo, ridicule, and vilification by members of his department who wanted to silence his views on intelligent design.
- Dr. Gonzalez's work on intelligent design was repeatedly attacked during the meetings in which his tenure was considered.
- Dr. Gonzalez's colleagues plotted to suppress evidence that could be used against them in court to provide proof of a hostile work environment.
- Dr. Gonzalez's department chair misled the public after the fact by trying to blame the denial of tenure on factors other than intelligent design.
- The majority of outside scientific advisors asked to consider Dr. Gonzalez's qualifications for the award of tenure recommended it, but his departmental colleagues ignored their recommendations.

The Discovery Institute summarizes this case as follows: "The bottom line according to these documents is that Dr. Gonzalez's rights to academic freedom, free speech, and a fair tenure process were trampled on by colleagues who were driven more by ideological zeal than by an impartial evaluation of Gonzalez's accomplishments as a scientist."[18]

WHY THE LEFT IS SO MILITANT IN ITS WAR AGAINST GOD, COUNTRY, AND CONSERVATIVES

The militancy of the Left in conducting its ideological war against God, country, and Conservatives is a by-product of its most widely adopted religious philosophy—secular humanism. Secular humanism, as practiced by the radical Left, holds that—among other things—man is naturally good or at least neutral rather than fallen in sin. If man is naturally good or even neutral, he is a product of his environment and can, therefore, be perfected by perfecting his environment.

Leftists don't understand or are unwilling to accept that perfection comes in the hereafter, not the here and now. In order to perfect man's environment—as if that could ever be achieved in a fallen world—it is necessary to know which environmental influences are good and which are bad. Members of the radical Left think they know which environmental influences are good and bad and they can distinguish between the two without any help from the Bible.

Hence, they attempt to bring good environmental influences to bear on individuals and society while eliminating the bad. This seems perfectly reasonable until you consider what it requires: 1) man not God decides what is good and bad, and 2) those *in the know*—Leftist ideologues—to have total control over all the factors influencing society. This means they must control government, the public schools, and, of course, higher education. In fact, education is the key to the whole enterprise because an educated person—as opposed to one who is indoctrinated—knows how to recognize nefarious motives, combat ignorance, question false beliefs, and reject forced attitudes. Such individuals are anathema to the Left.

If they can control education at all levels, Leftists can control the minds, beliefs, and attitudes of supposedly educated people. With this accomplished, perpetuating Leftist orthodoxy while silencing the views of those who oppose it is a much simpler task. Dissenting voices in education threaten the Left's monopoly and all of the things to be achieved by the Left for the Left. This is why the Left is so militant in carrying out its war against God, country, and Conservatives.

CHAPTER 8

FIGHTING BACK AGAINST MARXIST TYRANNY

Jordan B. Peterson, the author of *12 Rules for Life*, is among the most popular advocates (if book sales and followings are any indication) for traditional/biblical values due to his experience within the Canadian and American university system and the culture at large. In an interview with Joe Rogan, when addressing the solution to the Marxist influence in the academy, he offered a rather surprising answer:

> . . . there was an article in the *Boston Globe* this week saying the same thing that all of this crazy postmodern identity politics equality of outcome nonsense is not only disrupted the university, **in a way that might be irreparable as far as I can tell**, but it's rapidly spreading outside into the normal, say, business world . . . [emphasis mine].
>
> YouTube is the [new] university because there's hundreds of thousands of people on YouTube, maybe millions, who just want to learn. It's like, fine. I'm an educator. I'll talk to people who want to learn because if you're an educator that's

what you do. Is that most effectively done in the universities? Not self-evidently. And so, now I'm trying to figure this out.[1]

Could Peterson be right? Is the university system irrevocably broken? That, of course, remains to be seen and even if it can be repaired, we're looking at years, probably decades in the process. We must deal with the problem now and in a way that will safeguard our children and grandchildren. During the course of Peterson's interview with Joe Rogan, he also made a case for vocational or trade schools, so rather than expending a fortune to exit with an often valueless degree, students can emerge with marketable skills they can immediately put to revenue-generating work.

WHAT PARENTS CAN DO TO FIGHT BACK AGAINST MARXIST TYRANNY

Ensuring young Christians and Conservatives are able to get a college education rather than four years or more of Marxist indoctrination begins with parents. If we prepare our children well, even the most determined Marxists won't be able to transform them into Leftist ideologues who hate God, country, and the truth. What follows are specific steps parents can take to prepare their children for what awaits them in college:

- Begin by reading 1 Timothy chapter 1 carefully and then reading it again with your children. This chapter in Scripture is a warning against false teachers. Not only will this passage let young people know the types of things they may confront in college, it will let them know these things are false, destructive, and to be avoided.
- If there is a Christian college offering programs of study your children plan to pursue, give strong consideration

to this institution. Attending a Christian institution is no guarantee your children won't confront moral and ideological challenges during their college years, but if you check the school out carefully before settling on it you can at least reduce the challenges they will face.

- Do not be a helicopter parent. Prepare your children for life outside the home long before they leave home. This means giving them responsibilities to the family and holding them accountable for meeting their obligations. It also means letting them suffer the consequences of their bad behavior and bad decisions. Parents who do everything for their children while "protecting" them from the exigencies of life send them to college unprepared to deal with what they will face.

- Assess the spiritual and personal maturity of your children before allowing them to matriculate. Some high school graduates are ready to go away to college and some aren't. Do not allow or help your children to matriculate if they are not sufficiently mature both spiritually and personally to stand up to the challenges of college without being broken. If you have college-age children who still need to grow spiritually and personally, have them live at home and attend a local community college for their first two years or let them begin college online. Having them in the home will allow you to continue working on their spiritual and personal development. It will also give you opportunities to gauge how they are responding to the college experience and take appropriate action if what you see is not good.

- Don't automatically assume college is the best option for your children. It isn't for everyone. Young people who choose to go to college should have a definite purpose in mind such as a specific career field that cannot be achieved without a college degree. Students who don't yet know what they want to do with their lives should get a job or join the military. The last place your children need to go to "find themselves" is college. Students who go to college to find themselves invariably end up finding nothing but trouble. College is too expensive personally and financially for young people who choose to attend just because their friends are, they like the football team, or they just want to get away from their parents.

- Require your children to join a good church—one you check out—while in college. A good local church—especially one reaching out to college students—can be an anchor in a storm for young Christians facing the challenges of college life. It can also provide them a peer group to counter anti-Christian forces.
- Require your children to join a campus Christian organization while in college. This will ensure they can spend their out-of-class time with fellow believers and recharge their batteries after spending the day interacting with professors and students who reject God.
- Require your children to make home visits as often as possible while attending college. Monitor their attitudes and worldviews and act quickly if you detect creeping secularization. Better to remove your children from college than allow them to become Marxist minions who hate God, country, and truth.
- Require your children to work as soon as they are old enough and to save their earnings to help defray the costs of college. Then require them to work while in college. There time outside of class will be more wisely spent working and contributing to paying for college than in idle pursuits on campus.
- Discourage your children from taking out student loans to pay for college. Student loans just ensure they will start life after college in a deep financial hole.

WHAT CHURCHES CAN DO TO FIGHT BACK AGAINST MARXIST TYRANNY

Churches have an important role to play in helping parents and students fight back against Marxist tyranny. We emphasize this point because too many churches today have become places of entertainment rather than discipleship for young people. They have given into the culture and watered down their theology to accommodate rather than transform young people. As a result, instead of influencing the culture for Christ, they are influenced by the culture.

There is a role for the college student's home church and a role for churches in college and university towns. The home church should assist parents in bringing up their children in the instruction and admonition of Christ. Churches should reinforce what is taught in Christian homes and Christian parents should reinforce what is taught in church provided, of course, what is being taught in each setting is biblical.

In a sense, the home church should be a biblical bootcamp that helps parents prepare their children to function in a godly manner in an ungodly environment. Together parents and their church should give young people a solid foundation of faith so firmly instilled it cannot be undermined by Marxist professors. The home church can help by bringing in speakers who know what students can expect on college campuses. Christian students who are currently in college can be effective in helping prepare future college students for the challenges they will face. The home church can also help by providing special Bible studies or Sunday school classes for college-age students to teach them how to stand up to Marxist tyranny and the other challenges they will confront on campus.

Churches in college and university towns can play an important role by providing safe havens for Christian students, alternative social activities, and on-going counseling. They can also help by bringing college students together to pray and discuss the challenges they may be facing on campus. Pastors in these churches can play a critical role by establishing relationships with the parents of college students and giving them forewarning if they see their children drifting away from the faith.

WHAT INDIVIDUAL TAXPAYERS CAN DO TO FIGHT BACK AGAINST MARXIST TYRANNY

Even if you have no children in college, as a taxpayer, you still have a vested interest in what takes place on college and university campuses. The negatives associated with Marxist tyranny are not limited to those enrolled in college. Marxist professors are shaping the culture you live in, the government taxing you, the K-12 schools your children or grandchildren attend, the military protecting you, and the employer you work for. Fortunately, there are things you can do to minimize the damage Marxist professors inflict on the culture.

- Support the organizations protecting your freedoms. Two of the most effective are Alliance Defending Freedom (www.adflegal.org) and Summit Ministries (www.summit .org).
- Make sure your state legislators in the House and Senate as well as the members of Congress from your district and state know how you feel about Marxist tyranny in higher education. Public colleges and universities receive state and federal funding, meaning they receive your taxes. Let those who represent you at the state and national levels know you don't want your tax dollars used to support institutions that reject God and hate America.
- Support Christian education at all levels. Christian schools get no taxpayer support, yet they are the institutions

carrying the banner for Christ. After checking with local pastors and parents of children who attend the Christian school you plan to support to ensure it has not gone "woke" like the public schools, support the school even if you are not affiliated with it in any way.

- Make sure your church is engaged, that it is doing the things recommended in the previous section.
- Support Christian and conservative student organizations on college campuses even if you have no children or grandchildren in college.

WHAT STUDENTS CAN DO TO FIGHT BACK AGAINST MARXIST TYRANNY

The ultimate foot soldier in the fight against liberal tyranny in colleges and universities is **you**—the student. Like foot soldiers in every battle, you will bear the burden of standing eye to eye with the adversary every day and you, more than anyone else, will feel the heat of battle. Therefore, it is essential for you as a Christian and conservative student to know what you are up against and be prepared. For example, consider the case of California college student, Jonathan Lopez, who was verbally abused by his professor for daring to give a pro-marriage speech in class.

The context for this case of liberal tyranny is that just a month before Lopez gave his speech, California voters amended the state's constitution to protect traditional marriage. As part of his speech, Lopez read the dictionary definition of marriage. This was as far as he got. His professor stopped the class, called Lopez a "fascist b_ _ _ _ _d" and announced that anyone in class who was offended could leave. When the entire class chose to stay, the Leftist professor pre-empted Lopez by dismissing the class on the spot.[1]

Unfortunately, instances of abuse such as this are common in today's Marxist colleges and universities. This is why attaining a college degree is more difficult for Christian and conservative students than it is for non-believers. Not only will you have to satisfy the requirements of your professors and the institution, you will have to do so while defending yourself and your beliefs. Like any soldier, before engaging your adversary you need to: 1) be prepared, and 2) adopt effective strategies. Your preparation has been a lifelong endeavor that should have resulted in spiritual and personal maturity as well as a biblical worldview before you matriculated.

This chapter assumes you have developed the spiritual and personal maturity necessary to pursue a college education without losing your faith. We recommend students who have not reached this level of maturity to postpone college until they have. This chapter explains specific strategies you can use to succeed in a secular college or university without compromising your Christian and conservative principles:

- Know who God is
- Know what to expect
- Be part of campus life without being compromised by it
- Use critical thinking as a tool in refuting the false and/or misguided views of the Left
- Fight back, but do so in a spirit of Christian love
- Stand up to temptation
- Persevere against liberal tyranny in all its forms
- Go on the offensive against liberal tyranny.

Know Who God Is

Before stepping foot on a college or university campus, get straight in your mind who God is and who you are. This is critical because you will be entering an environment that rejects God or, at the very least, distorts who He is. God is your Lord and Savior. It is God, not professors, not fellow students, and not the world you should seek to please and to emulate. It is God, not professors, who will ultimately determine the trajectory of your life on earth and whether or not you will enjoy eternal life thereafter.

Before going away to college, we recommend you memorize either the Apostles' Creed or the Nicene Creed and make sure you know what every word of the creed you choose means. You may have grown up reciting one of these creeds in church. You might even be able to recite one of them word for word right now. But do you really understand what the words mean? Do not go away to college until you do. Ask your pastor for help if need be.

Knowing who God is and that you are His child can make the difference between succeeding not just in college but in life in a world increasingly rejecting God. Knowing who God is and you are a child of God can keep you centered in times of emotional and intellectual turmoil; the kinds of times you will certainly experience in college. In everything you think, do, and say during your college years—and thereafter—seek to please God. In every situation you face, seek to obey God. Do this and you will not just survive your college experience, you will thrive in it.

Know What to Expect

A good description of the modern college or university campus is *Disney World without the rides*. Like the Magic Kingdom, the university campus bears little resemblance to the real world. It is a one-of-a-kind environment like nothing you have ever experienced and never will again after college. The modern campus can seem like an alien environment, especially to Christian and conservative students. Therefore, it is important to know what to expect before you matriculate. What follows are some of the emotions, feelings, and fears you are likely to experience early in your college career:

- *Homesickness.* For many new students, going away to college is the first time they have been away from their families for an extended period. Moving outside of your comfort zone—family, friends, church, and familiar surroundings—can be disconcerting for even the most eager college student. Consequently, homesickness is a common reaction for new college students. Rather than fret about it, take your homesickness as a reminder of what is important in life. Look at college as temporary, but your family and relationship with God as permanent. Stay in touch with your family throughout your time in college and join a good church in the community near your campus so you have a church family to lean on for support.

- *Alienation.* Christian and conservative students often feel they have landed on an alien planet when first arriving on campus. For students raised in a Christian environment, a university campus can seem like a strange new world where anything and everything goes. Much of what you will observe on campus will be at odds with how you have been raised. As a result, you are likely to feel alienated from the crowd. Drinking, drugs, immodest dress, foul language, recreational sex, aggressive homosexuality, and transgenderism, as well as other forms of openly flaunted immorality may seem like the norm. Whatever forms of worldly behavior are practiced in secular culture will be seen on a university campus and magnified in both frequency and intensity. The key for Christian and conservative students is to remember you are to be in the world but not of it. In fact, if you stop feeling alienated during your college years, there may be a problem.

- *Loneliness.* Christian and conservative college students often feel alone in the midst of a crowd. Although there are plenty of students on campus, they are so different in their worldviews and personal habits it may be difficult for you to relate to them. Consequently, one of the first things you will want to do after arriving on campus is join a Christian and a conservative student organization. This will allow you to interact with other students who share your values and understand your concerns, vulnerabilities, and fears.

- *Besieged.* Christian and conservative students often feel as if they are under attack by professors and fellow students who disagree with their views and are openly hostile to them. If you feel this way, you are right; you are under attack. This fact is precisely why we wrote this book. The remainder of this chapter is devoted to helping you learn how to fight back, break through the siege of Marxist tyranny, and emerge the victor.

Be Part of Campus Life without Being Compromised by It

Christians understand the challenge of being in the world without being of it. Having to meet this challenge should not be new to you. Christians certainly don't escape this situation by going to college. In fact, college just increases the magnitude of the problem. Almost everything about the world Christians should avoid being part of can be readily found on a university campus. The key to this strategy is learning how to interact in a positive way with non-believers while not being seduced by their views or changed by their behavior.

- *Remember at all times who you are and what you believe.* You will not be on campus long before opportunities to do things you shouldn't do will present themselves. Opportunities to drink, use drugs, cheat on school work, engage in recreational sex, and participate in other forms of sinful behavior will abound during your college years. No matter what you see the crowd doing, remember at all times who you are and what you believe. Do not hide your Christianity to avoid offending others. Fellow students who would lead you astray aren't worthy of your concern. Further, do not underestimate the power of your positive example to influence weak students who are just going along to get along. Your refusal to participate in the wrong kinds of activities might give another person the determination to refuse. On the other hand, if a student who knows you are a Christian sees you going along with the crowd, he might use your poor example as "permission" to go along too. Remember, you are a child of God committed to following the example of Jesus Christ, and you know right from wrong. Be prepared during your college years to follow the advice made famous by Nancy Reagan: "Just say NO."

- *Join Appropriate Student Organizations.* You will soon learn even the strongest Christians and the most dedicated Conservatives need the support of like-minded individuals during their college years. One of the best ways to establish a base of support right away after arriving on campus is to join an appropriate student organization. You can quickly determine which organizations are available on campus by visiting the Student Activities office at your institution. Typically available campus student organizations include the following: Young America's Foundation, Students for Academic Freedom, Baptist Collegiate Ministry, Campus Outreach, Fellowship of Christian Athletes, InterVarsity Christian Fellowship, Presbyterian Student Organization, Reformed University Fellowship, Wesley Foundation, and a variety of others supported by specific denominations. These organizations can provide a friendly environment in which to recharge your intellectual and spiritual batteries, gain respite from your daily battles with Leftist activists,

and interact with others who share your beliefs and challenges. A word of caution here: As we are all too aware,
organizations can drift from their founding principles
and values. Be sure to investigate before you join.

- *Be a witness for Christ.* Every Christian should be an evan-
gelist. We are called not just to know God, but to help
others know God. If you join a Christian student organization, it will probably organize campus activities in
which you can participate. But you do not have to wait
for activities sponsored by Christian organizations. By
your example you can be a witness for Christ every day.
Even the most ardently atheistic college professor will
notice the example of a Christian student who is always:
1) in class on time, 2) well-prepared, and 3) first to turn
in required assignments. Even Leftist professors who
reject your views will appreciate your diligence. Further,
your fellow students will notice: 1) your example of artic-
ulating your views in a calm and reasoned manner, 2) the
fact you are thoroughly prepared and know your subject
well, 3) your ability to disagree without being disagreeable, 4) your steadfastness in persisting in your beliefs
even when browbeaten by a Marxist professor, and
5) your perseverance in continuing to swim upstream
against the current of Leftist orthodoxy. This is why no
matter how poorly your professors or fellow students
behave, your response must always be tempered by
Christian love.

Use Critical Thinking as a Tool for Refuting the False Claims of the Left

The Achilles' heel of Marxists is logic. Their views are built
on a foundation of sand. One of the best ways to refute the
assertions of a Marxist is by taking the assertions out to their
logical conclusions. For example, one of the foundational
planks in the platform of the Left is what they call

"pro-choice," by which they mean pro-abortion. The reason pro-abortion advocates insist an unborn baby is not a human being is where logic leads if they admit the obvious fact of its humanity. If an unborn baby is a human being rather than just a "fetus," logic makes clear pro-abortion advocates support killing for the sake of convenience. If this is the case, can the elderly, homeless, mentally disabled, and others among us who at times are inconvenient be killed too? Logic would say "yes." This is just one example of why it is important for you to develop critical thinking skills. By thinking critically, you can find the holes in the arguments of Marxists, point them out, and refuse to be swayed by them.

What Is Critical Thinking? Critical thinking involves applying sound reasoning, good judgment, and objective logic when analyzing and interpreting the input of others. Critical thinking will help you recognize bias in the arguments of others, assess the motives behind the views professed by others, distinguish between facts and opinions, distinguish between explanations and rationalizations, recognize fundamental issues, distinguish between causes and symptoms, and use facts to eliminate the fog of ambiguity.[2]

Differences Between Critical Thinkers and Non-Critical Thinkers. Non-critical thinkers tend to be closed-minded, inflexible, and stubborn when discussing issues. You are probably going to experience these characteristics firsthand during your college years. For example, these traits describe the professor in the example cited at the beginning of this chapter when Jonathan Lopez was profanely interrupted and his pro-marriage speech cut short by a professor who displayed anything but critical thinking skills. Non-critical thinkers also tend to be overly confident and arrogant about their views. Once again you will probably experience this during your college years. Non-critical thinkers often react on the basis of emotion rather than intellectual curiosity or scholarly inquiry.

Because of their manifest failings as critical thinkers, some Marxist professors resort to verbal abuse, intimidation, and persecution when interacting with Christian and conservative students and colleagues. Some of the best examples of this phenomenon are found in the debates raging on university campuses about intelligent design. Opponents of intelligent design are typically highly educated scholars who have gained a measure of credibility among their colleagues. Since this is the case, one would expect in debating advocates of intelligent design they would be able to calmly and rationally explain why they disagree with the concept. Instead, the Darwinists often stoop to the kind of name calling, mudslinging, and dirty tactics associated with old-fashioned, big-city politics. By using tactics so pointedly at odds with what one would expect of highly educated scholars, Marxists damage their own credibility in the long run.

Overcoming the Faulty Reasoning of Rabid Marxist and Secular Humanists. As a critical thinker in a Marxist university, you will often find yourself having to deal with the faulty reasoning of Leftist ideologues who are so determined to advance their anti-God, anti-conservative agenda their scholarly logic is supplanted by visceral emotion. What follows are some common manifestations of this phenomenon. As a critical thinker, you should prepare yourself to recognize the errors in logic of Leftist ideologues and be prepared to point them out during discussions and debates. Feldman lists the following tactics and errors of non-critical thinkers:[3]

- *Introducing irrelevant information.* Assume your class is discussing the issue of gun control. Your professor, arguing the Second Amendment should be rescinded, says,

"The Founding Fathers did not anticipate the development of assault weapons like AK-47s with thirty-round magazines." As a critical thinker, you could point out the irrelevance of his argument by explaining the relative capabilities of different weapons had nothing to do with the original deliberations about the Second Amendment. Rather, the Founding Fathers were determined to ensure citizens would always have the right and the ability to defend themselves and their families. The context for the Second Amendment was the Founders' fear of an armed military force being imposed on American citizens as the British troops were prior to the War for Independence, not the firepower of the weapons available to Americans at any given time.

- *Oversimplifying.* Assume the discussion in your class is about the immoral practice of abortion. Your professor, who is an ardent pro-abortionist, says: "It's a woman's body we are talking about. I should be able to do what I want with my body." As a critical thinker, you could point out the oversimplification in her argument by explaining how abortion is not just something a woman does with her body like getting a tattoo or applying makeup. Further, there is more involved than just her body, such as the life of the child and the coarsening of society that comes with such practices as abortion.

- *Arguing from ignorance.* Assume the discussion in your dormitory is about service in the military. A fellow student says, "I will never serve in the military. All they do is teach you how to kill innocent women and children." As a critical thinker, you could point out this student is arguing from ignorance. First, he has never served in the military so he has no basis for making such a claim. Second, had he ever served or had he studied the question in even a cursory manner, he would know better.

- *Using circular reasoning.* Circular reasoning is reasoning supported only by itself. Assume you are discussing the concept of universal healthcare with some friends in the student union. An advocate of the concept says, "We should adopt universal healthcare right now. It is the best way to provide healthcare in a civilized society." When another student inquires as to the basis for this assertion, the universal healthcare advocate says, "I just know it's the right thing to do." You could point out this is circular reasoning. Because it has no basis in fact, it raises many questions but answers none.
- *Using the destructive ad hominem argument.* This is the favorite tactic of the radical Left. It means when you cannot refute your opponent's argument, attack your opponent or his character (bearing false witness against your neighbor). The case of the California professor who called Jonathan Lopez a "fascist b_ _ _ _ _d" during his speech in favor of traditional marriage is an example of the destructive ad hominem argument taken to an extreme—an increasingly common practice on university campuses. Had you been a student in Lopez's class, you could have pointed out the professor's opinion of the student's parentage was irrelevant. Lopez advocated a specific point of view in his speech, one that California voters showed their overwhelming support for at the ballot box. If the professor disagreed, he should have refuted the student's point of view—if he could—or offered an alternative. Attacking the student instead of his opinion—using the destructive ad hominem argument—is beneath the dignity of a college professor.
- *Using the slippery slope argument.* The slippery slope argument suggests taking a certain action will automatically lead to an ever-worsening set of circumstances. The twisted logic behind this argument is: "Give them an inch

and they will take a mile." Darwinists use this argument in their attempts to silence creationists and advocates of intelligent design. Assume your class is discussing Darwinism versus creationism. Your professor angrily asserts, "Give Christians an inch in this battle and they will turn our universities into a bunch of church schools!" As a critical thinker, you could point out the professor is using the slippery slope argument. Giving Christians opportunities to advocate on behalf of their beliefs without fear of persecution is a long way from converting public universities into "church schools."

- *Using inflammatory language.* It's a sad commentary this has become a favored tactic of the radical Left in colleges and universities. Like using the ad hominem argument, using inflammatory language is an act of emotion fueled by desperation. When Darwinists refer to creationists as "stupid" or when advocates of homosexual marriage refer to Christians as "fascists," they are using this tactic. Assume your class is discussing the case presented earlier in this book in which Guillermo Gonzalez was denied tenure because of his views on intelligent design. Your professor continually refers to Dr. Gonzalez using such inflammatory terms as "moron" and "idiot." As a critical thinker, you could point out that calling a fellow professor with the credentials of Dr. Gonzalez such names is inflammatory and hardly what you would expect from a college professor. If you really wanted to challenge your Left-leaning professor, you might ask him how his credentials compare with those of Dr. Gonzalez and ask what that says about his being a moron or an idiot.

- *Using intimidating language.* This has become another favored tactic of the radical Left on university campuses. It works like this. If you cannot refute opponents' views with logic, reason, or facts, use intimidation to prevent them from stating those views. Assume your class is

discussing the issue of stem cell research. A Christian
student raises several questions about the ethics of it. The
professor responds by saying, "Anyone in this class who
holds your views is not likely to pass." As a critical thinker,
you could point out this is blatant intimidation, a practice
at odds with the scholarly approach and the professed
concept of academic freedom.

- *Appealing to compassion.* One of the ploys of the radical
  Left, especially when trying to convert naïve Christians
  who may not be as well-versed in their own beliefs as they
  should be, is to appeal to compassion. After all, as Christians shouldn't we follow Christ's example of compassion? Assume your class is discussing the issue of allowing
  homosexual couples to adopt children. Your professor
  says, "How could anyone possibly object to this when the
  gay couple will be good parents who will provide a loving
  and supportive home for these poor abandoned children?" As a critical thinker, you might point out the
  professor is astutely but disingenuously using compassion
  to gain the support of his listeners without providing the
  whole story. His argument on behalf of the "poor abandoned children" has an obvious shortcoming: it assumes
  the children in question cannot be adopted by Christians
  or other parents who would also provide them a "loving
  and supportive home" without all of the confusion and
  sociocultural stress inherent in a homosexual adoption.
- *Using ridicule.* Marxist professors are especially enamored
  of this tactic because it can be used on Christian and
  conservative students without stepping over the line into
  blatant persecution or abuse. The point of the tactic is to
  embarrass those who hold different views so they will be
  reluctant to express them in the future. Assume your class
  is discussing the issue of whether America should rein-
  state the draft (mandatory military service). A military
  veteran in your class says, "I joined the Army right after

graduating from high school and it was an outstanding experience for me. I think people who oppose the draft might change their minds if they gave military service a chance." Your professor responds with a derisive laugh and says, "Come now, surely you can see how infantile your opinion is. I don't have to murder someone to know I don't want to do it." As a critical thinker, you might point out: 1) ridiculing an idea is not the same as refuting it, 2) killing someone is not necessarily murder, and 3) in a scholarly environment an idea should remain on the table until it can be refuted—if it can be refuted.

Recognizing the tactics of the radical Left explained in this section will help when you are subjected to them. When you stand your ground against a Marxist professor, other students, or anyone else using these tactics, remember who you are. Fight back but do so in a spirit of Christian love. Methods for fighting back without stooping to the tactics of the Left are explained in the next section.

Fight Back in a Spirit of Christian Love

As you read in the previous section, Marxists, secular humanists, atheists, and agnostics will go to great lengths and use disturbing tactics in their attempts to silence Christian and conservative voices on university campuses. In fact, the radical Left has shown a willingness to be blatantly mean-spirited in attacking the worldviews of Christians and Conservatives. When this happens to you, the desire to verbally blast your attacker with both barrels is an understandable human reaction. However, like many human reactions, this is one you will need to suppress through prayer and self-discipline.

As a Christian you have a higher level of responsibility in these situations than your secular counterparts. In attempting to advance their views, any tactic that works is acceptable to the radical Left. This is not the case with Christians. We too must profess our views and defend them with vigor, but we are called to do these things in a spirit of Christian love. God expects us to speak His truth, but in doing so He expects us to reflect the righteousness of His Son. Consequently, you will need to become skilled in the art and science of disagreeing with others without being disagreeable and speaking hard truths in love. The following methods will help:

- *Be prepared.* Know your Bible and what it says about the issues of the day—those likely to come up in classroom and campus discussions. The radical Left has become adept at using the biblical ignorance of some Christians against them by distorting what the Bible says, taking verses out of context, misapplying verses, and asking believers questions from Scripture they cannot answer. The Bible is a tool God has given us so we can know Him and help others know Him. Don't let your ignorance of it allow the radical Left to use it as a weapon against you.
- *Listen more, talk less.* You learn more from listening than from talking. The beliefs of Marxists are self-defeating by their very nature. Stripped down to their essentials, these beliefs are built on one simple premise: man is God and, more specifically, each individual is his or her own god. Consequently, the beliefs of the Left depend on circular reasoning for their validity. If you listen carefully, you will find Marxists almost always end up arguing against themselves, especially when they base their assumptions on the concept of moral relativism. You may have heard the maxim about *giving a fool enough rope to hang himself.* This is what you do when you listen to Marxists profess their secular humanist opinions. Listen long enough and the Marxist will eventually give you opportunities for rebuttal

big enough to sail an ocean liner through. This is an effective method for dealing with Marxists, but it is made even more effective by the fact there is another method buried within it. Everyone likes a good listener. This is especially true of the many academicians who chose higher education as a profession because it gives them a podium and a built-in audience. If you come to be known as a good listener, you will eventually have an abundance of opportunities to share your views with Leftist ideologues who can benefit from them.

- *Use discretion.* You have only so many arrows in your quiver. Consequently, when going into battle, choose your targets with care and for greatest effect. You do not have to take on every Leftist ideologue who says something you disagree with. Do this in today's campus environment and you will spend every waking moment debating with Marxists instead of seeing to your studies. Sometimes you have to just ignore Marxists. It is better to carefully select high impact opportunities in which advocating or defending your views will have the greatest effect. Use the discernment offered by the Holy Spirit.

- *Be patient.* Your run-ins with Marxists on campus, as important as they are to you, are really just small skirmishes in a much larger battle. Further, these larger battles are just part of an even larger sociocultural war the Left is waging on God, country, and Conservatives in America. Don't think you have to win the war all by yourself. Be patient. Sometimes the best way to deal with Marxists is to ignore them. Further, when you do engage Leftist professors and students be patient enough to listen to them. Sometimes the best way to handle Marxists is to simply pray for them. When you do this, don't expect immediate results but never doubt what God can do.

- *Pray before engaging.* When you decide to engage a Leftist ideologue in a discussion or debate, slow down. Before jumping in with both feet, take the time to say a silent prayer. Ask God for strength, guidance, and the proper motivation. Ask Him to help you reflect the image of His Son as you discuss the issue in question. Winning another convert to Christ is even more important than winning an argument with a Marxist.

- *Control your temper.* As a Christian, if you lose your temper when debating a Marxist, you lose the debate and your credibility. Often it will be the manner of your speech that brings Leftist ideologues around rather than your words. If you feel your temper rising, take a deep breath, say a quick prayer, and do not respond until you regain control of your emotions. This tactic is the key to being able to disagree without being disagreeable.

- *Commit to disagreeing without being disagreeable.* If you find yourself thinking, *I am going to show this Marxist so-and-so what's what*, stop and examine your motivation. In any conflict with Leftist professors and students, your first motivation should be to reflect the image of Christ. Defend your position with vigor but do so with grace and concern for your adversaries. Attack their opinions, but do not attack them. The radical Left is determined to stifle Christians and Conservatives as part of its campaign for intellectual and ideological conformity and supremacy. When subjected to persecution by the radical Left, you are likely to become angry. When this happens, take a deep breath, say a prayer, and remember that anger will not help you reflect the image of Christ or persuade your adversary of the validity of your opinions.

Stand Up to Temptation

Much of what you will be subjected to in a university environment will run counter to your Christian worldview. There will be opportunities to engage all kinds of behavior that runs contrary to God's will and your benefit. You will be tempted by such factors as peer pressure, curiosity, and the desire to taste forbidden fruit. In these cases, your worst enemy is your own sinful nature. Remember, temptation is Satan's way of appealing to your sinful nature to lure you into doing things you shouldn't.

The first step in standing up to temptation is admitting you are vulnerable to it. One of the ways Christian college students get into trouble is by thinking they are immune to the temptations of the world. Christian college students sometimes think their faith is strong enough they can watch R and X-rated movies and not be tempted by portrayed sex and violence, or hang out with friends who use drugs and not be affected. These students mistakenly think they can walk through a pigsty without getting mud on their shoes. Maybe some Christians can do these things and not be changed, but most cannot. Christians are just like anyone else in that we have a sinful nature and Satan knows how to use it to tempt us into doing what we shouldn't.

Standing up to the ever-present temptations on college and university campuses will require a concerted effort on your part. What follows are some strategies that will help:

- *Observe others and learn from their mistakes.* A smart man learns from his mistakes, but a wise man learns from the mistakes of others. As you stand up to campus temptations, be wise and learn from the mistakes of others. When you see a fellow Christian student give in to temptation, ask yourself: "In the same situation, what could I have done to avoid his mistake?" Correspondingly, when you see fellow Christian students successfully turn away from temptation, make note of how they did it, learn from the experience, and congratulate them.
- *Minimize the temptations you are subjected to.* Avoid temptation intensive activities and events. Agreeing to hang

out in a bar, attend parties where you know drugs will be used, or spend time alone in a dorm room or apartment with a friend of the opposite sex are the types of decisions that increase the amount of temptation you will be subjected to. A wiser approach is to minimize your exposure to temptation by refusing to participate in these types of temptation intensive activities. This is the message in 2 Timothy 2:22: "So flee youthful passions and pursue righteousness, faith, love, and peace, along with those who call on the Lord from a pure heart."

- *Use the Bible as your armor against temptation.* When you find yourself being pulled in the wrong direction by temptation, put on the brakes long enough to open your Bible. Find a quiet place and start reading. Focus on verses dealing with temptation. Begin with Matthew 4: 1–11 where Christ turns away from the temptations of Satan. Continue this exercise until the urge to give into temptation passes.

- *Fortify your heart with prayer.* Few things will stop Satan in his tracks so effectively as the prayers of a believer. If you feel pulled in the wrong direction by temptation, fortify your heart with prayer, and Satan will flee from you. This is what is meant in James 4:7: "Therefore submit to God. Resist the devil, and he will flee from you." A good place to begin is with the Lord's Prayer. Remember this prayer says: ". . . and lead us not into temptation, but deliver us from evil" (Matt. 6:13).

- *Do not try to fight temptation alone.* As a Christian you are never alone. Remember this when you must stand up to temptation. God is there and He will help if you go to Him in prayer. In addition, you can find support in an accountability partner. This is another Christian you can contact when temptation is getting the upper hand. Your accountability partner is someone you can count on to help you do the right thing. Being a member of a

Christian student organization will give you opportunities to find an accountability partner and to be one for other Christian students.

Persevere against Marxist Tyranny in All Its Forms

Some Christian and conservative students retreat into a shell and hide their worldviews to avoid the abuse of Left-leaning college professors. Some simply drop out of college. Every time a Christian or conservative college student chooses to retreat in these and other ways, the radical Left wins a victory. Standing up to the adversity you face in college will not be easy, but doing so will strengthen you for the even bigger culture war awaiting you after college. Marxist tyranny on campus is the focus of this book, but Marxist tyranny is not restricted to college and university campuses. It permeates American society. Consequently, one of the most important lessons you can learn in college is how to persevere against it.

Stand Up to Adversity. As a Christian or Conservative in an institution dominated by the Left, take it as a given you will experience adversity. This fact should be understood before deciding to pursue a college education. Learning how to stand up to adversity is critical to your success in college. Those who lose faith when they encounter roadblocks, detours, and potholes on the road to success are destined to fail. Never view yourself as a victim; victims are never victors.

According to Pastor Voddie Baucham Jr., "The Christian life that is void of suffering has never experienced real growth. It has never seen the end of itself and the remarkable grace of the intervening hand of God. It has never done the undoable, seen the unimaginable, or received the unattainable. The Christian life that has not seen suffering does not truly know that God is able, that He is good, that He is always right on time, that He is larger than our greatest fears, that He is nearer than the wind on our faces."[4]

Since adversity is likely to be part of your college experience, you must know how to stand up to it. The following strategies will help:

- *Remember God has a purpose for your suffering.* God uses adversity to strengthen His saints, as is shown in Romans 5:3–5: "We rejoice in our sufferings, knowing that suffering produces endurance, and endurance produces character, and character produces hope, and hope does not put us to shame." Learning to stand up to the adversity you experience in college is part of God's plan to strengthen you for even bigger challenges in the future.
- *Use adversity to get you closer to God.* Never make the mistake of letting adversity drive a wedge between you and God. Frustrated Christian students sometimes feel as if college would be a breeze were it not for their beliefs. This is why some hide their beliefs during college. This is a mistake. Let the challenges of pursuing a college education in a Leftist university drive you closer to God. As humans we are frail, but with God we can gain the strength to persevere.
- *Remember you are not alone in your adversity.* When you have just endured a distasteful encounter with an overbearing Leftist professor, it is easy to think you are alone. You are not. There may be other like-minded students in your class who are afraid to speak out. There are certainly others on campus. Second Timothy 3:12 says: "All who desire to live a godly life in Christ Jesus will be persecuted." Seek out fellow Christians on campus who have suffered because of their faith but persevered, learn from their experience, and grow from their wisdom. This is one of the reasons we recommend you join a Christian student organization while in college. These

organizations will bring you together on a regular basis with Christians who are facing or have faced the same challenges you are facing. Just knowing you are not alone can bolster your spirit and your resolve.

- *Refuse to give in to adversity.* Use the Bible, prayer, the power of the Holy Spirit, and the suffering of others to keep the adversity you face in college in proper perspective. Doing this will give you the strength to keep going when you feel like giving up. God is bigger than the problems you face in college. He knows what you are up against and how much you can take. God is like the coach who knows athletes must suffer through the pain of being pushed to their physical, mental, and emotional limits if they are going to excel and improve. Rely on God to be your coach during times of adversity; He knows your limits.

- *Reach out to someone else who is being persecuted.* One of the best ways to help yourself during times of adversity is to help someone else. Invariably, when we reach out to others who are carrying burdens, we gain a more positive and thankful perspective. No matter how much we are suffering, there are others who are hurting even more. In times of adversity, during your college years and after, help yourself by helping others. We are not talking about living by comparisons; we are encouraging you to take godly leadership roles, formal and informal.

- *Take the long view.* In times of adversity, it is easy to get caught up in the pain of the moment and think your problems will never end. They will. Consequently, it helps to take the long view. When you feel like the pressure to conform to a liberal worldview will never end, remember what it says in Romans 8:28: "And we know that for those who love God all things work together for good, for those who are called according to his purpose."

Cling to God in times of trouble and you will eventually emerge from it stronger and better. Remember, trusting in yourself has a short and painful limit; trusting in your heavenly Father is temporal and eternal security. Look up 1 John 4:4 and store it in your heart and mind for regular referral.

Go on Offensive against Marxist Tyranny. Christians in secular settings spend a lot of time defending their faith, and Conservatives in settings dominated by Marxists spend a lot of time defending their beliefs. When we served in the Marine Corps, we were taught the following maxim: *The best defense is a strong offense.* We learned you should never just sit back and take what the enemy throws at you. Instead, turn the tables on your adversary by going on the offensive. What follows are some strategies for this purpose:

- Engage the Left in debates
- Start a Conservative student organization or take a biblically strong position as a leader
- Host Christian and conservative speakers and events.

Engage the Left in Debates. The radical Left functions best when it can broadcast one-way tirades against God, country, and Conservatives. Inflicting uncontested diatribes on a captive audience is easy. Anyone can win a one-sided fight. But things are different when Leftist ideologues and students are challenged and must defend their views. This is one of the reasons the radical Left wants to silence Christian and conservative college students. Engaging the Left in debates is an effective way to go on the offensive, but in order for this strategy to bear fruit you must be well prepared. Never go into battle unarmed and unprepared. Bay Buchanan recommends the following tactics for engaging the Left in debate:[5]

- *Define your goal.* Do not undertake a debate without first deciding what you want to accomplish. Do you want to convert your opponent, impress the audience, balance the discussion, antagonize the opposition, or just make sure the Christian and conservative point of view is heard? Do you want to reveal the shortcomings of Marxism, secular humanism, and moral relativism? Your goal determines the approach you will take in the debate.
- *Use nonverbal communication to your best advantage.* A substantial part of communication is nonverbal. One of the reasons Vice-President Nixon did better on the radio than on television when debating John F. Kennedy during the presidential election of 1960 was listeners could not see him. Those who watched the debate on television observed Nixon sending all the wrong nonverbal messages. He did not smile and so appeared mean-spirited. He kept furtively glancing at Kennedy instead of maintaining eye contact with the audience. He fidgeted and appeared nervous. Declining professional help with his makeup, Nixon appeared haggard and in need of a shave. All of these nonverbal mistakes hurt him. But on the radio, listeners gave Nixon the edge over Kennedy because they were not distracted by negative nonverbal messages. When you debate someone, remember these nonverbal tactics: 1) look at the audience, 2) maintain a friendly demeanor or at least a non-aggressive one, 3) speak with conviction about your beliefs (passive, disinterested monotones are not persuasive, but on the other hand neither are loud, boisterous, or mean-spirited comments), 4) stand up straight and make a conscious effort to avoid nervous affectations (uh, um, jiggling change in your pockets, white-knuckling the podium), 5) use self-effacing humor when possible, but avoid humor that puts down or embarrasses your opponent,

and 6) dress up for the occasion (this will show respect for the audience, the issues, and your opponent).

- *Prepare, prepare, prepare.* Never go into battle unarmed. Study the issues to be debated from your point of view and from your opponent's. Ideally you should know your opponent's views and facts better than he or she does. Further, you should know your side of the issue so well your opponent cannot use the same tactic on you.

- *Avoid drowning the audience in facts and figures.* Having a few carefully selected facts and figures ready to use at an appropriate moment is good debating strategy. However, drowning the audience and opponents in a tidal wave of facts will just win *them* points with listeners. Use enough facts to show you know your topic, but not so many you sound like an accountant talking to the IRS. Audiences respond better to illustrative stories than to long recitations of data.

- *Make an outline of key points and reminders.* An outline will help you stay focused and on message. Do not try to memorize what you plan to say. There are several reasons for this: 1) you will get nervous and forget, 2) you will sound stiff and scripted, and 3) your opponent might catch you off guard by introducing information not covered in your script. It is better to appear natural, well-informed, and comfortable with your material.

- *Speak from the heart.* If you don't appear to believe in your views, why should the audience? Don't overdo it but show the audience—verbally and nonverbally—you are interested in what you are saying and believe it to be the truth.

- *Practice before engaging.* A bright general once said even the best plan will not survive contact with the enemy. Another way to express the same principle is things seldom turn out exactly the way you think they will. Flexibility is an important asset for debaters. It allows you to be quick on your feet, or at least appear to be. Some people are naturally this way, but most are not. This is why it is important to practice often before actually engaging in debate. By practice, we mean discussing the issues to be debated with fellow Christians and Conservatives and asking them to play the role of the opposition. In presidential debates, both candidates practice by having staff members and other experts pose the questions they think the opposition might raise during the debate. You don't want to get caught flat-footed during a debate and have to admit, "I never thought of that."

Start a Conservative Student Organization. Most universities have Christian student organizations, but this is not the case with conservative student organizations. If your university does not have a student organization dedicated to advancing a conservative worldview, start one. We recommend affiliating with an established national organization. This approach can provide several advantages including access to services, training, speakers, publications, publicity, by-laws, and conferences. It also provides a national support base, invaluable in assisting with both startup challenges and ongoing operations. The national conservative student organization we recommend is Young America's Foundation:

Young America's Foundation
110 Elden Street
Herndon, Virginia 20170
http://www.yaf.org

Host Christian and Conservative Speakers and Events. Universities frequently host special events with prominent speakers from different fields. Exposing students to the diverse views of leading thinkers from different fields is part of what a university is supposed to do. Further, participating in these types of events is supposed to be part of the college experience for students. However, in universities dominated by Marxists, special events with speakers are typically designed to advance their Leftist agenda. The majority of these events on most university campuses support the causes of the radical Left (e.g., gun control, abortion, gay rights, etc.). One of the best ways to fight back against Marxist tyranny is to organize campus events with Christian and conservative speakers.

If your university does not provide balance in the special events it offers, do it yourself. Not only is this a good way to fight back, it will enhance your education and that of your fellow students. If you are a member of a Christian or conservative student organization, it can be helpful in organizing events and arranging speakers. This is one of the reasons we recommend joining or starting student organizations with a national affiliation. The key is to begin by identifying your institution's procedures for organizing events and inviting speakers. Know the bureaucracy and how it works. If you are a Christian or conservative student, dealing with your university should be approached like dealing with the IRS— know their rules better than they do. The university may try to passively kill your proposed event by burying it in red tape and paperwork.

The university's guidelines for organizing special events are published in either its catalog or its student handbook. Follow established procedures to the letter. Do not let haphazard planning on your part give the university a legitimate reason to deny approval of the proposed event. Be persistent and do not back down or give up. If you find yourself dealing with an obstructive university official who is obviously trying to block the event in spite of your having followed established procedures, contact the national chapter of your student organization or Alliance Defending Freedom (adflegal.org).

As a college student, you are on the front line in the fight against Marxist tyranny on campus. If this sounds daunting, just keep in mind the material explained in this chapter. You can survive your college experience with your Christian and conservative worldview unscathed provided you know what to expect and respond appropriately. Responding appropriately means being a critical thinker, standing up to temptation, persevering, fighting back in a spirit of Christian love, committing to being a part of campus life without compromising your principles, and going on the offensive. Do these things and you will not just survive the fight with the radical Left, you will win it. Having said this, do not get so absorbed in fighting back against Marxist tyranny you neglect your studies. Never give the Left ammunition in the form of bad grades and incomplete classes. You will have more credibility with your fellow Christians, Conservatives, undecided students, and the Left if you excel as a student. You will have more influence with the university when you are one of their alumni.

A FINAL WORD ON MARXIST TYRANNY IN HIGHER EDUCATION

The sociocultural decline in our country since the end of World War II is deeply disturbing. In every aspect of American life, the radical Left has made inroads leading our country farther and farther down a one-way street to destruction. Rick Scarborough accurately sums up the current situation in America in his book *Enough Is Enough* where he writes:

> America needs a healing. The evidence of that need is everywhere you turn now: failing schools, rampant immorality, broken homes, violent crime, exploitation of children, pornography, a faltering economy, loss of jobs—all leading to growing despair and hopelessness. Empowered by their many successes over the past seventy years and the inability of the Right to stop them, the Left is now ready to move in for the final solution: the criminalization of Christianity and the silencing of the confessing church.[1]

One of the principal battlegrounds in the radical Left's war against God, country, and Conservatives is the university campus. It is where Marxist faculties—aided and abetted by university administrators—make their most concerted efforts to dominate American society. Their strategies include: 1) giving the most radical elements of the Left an open microphone while drowning out the voices of Christians and Conservatives, 2) using pressure, intimidation, persecution, and abuse to promote intellectual conformity while discouraging any and all scholarly inquiry that runs counter to Leftist orthodoxy, 3) using secular humanism disguised as scholarship to turn Christian and conservative students away from their core beliefs, 4) turning naïve young people who have never learned to think critically into Marxist minions, and 5) using their position of dominance to silence Christian and conservative thought, scholarship, opinions, and dissent.

In September 2021, Professor Peter Boghossian of Portland State University decided enough was enough and resigned. In his letter of resignation, Boghossian claimed the university's administration created an environment that punished dissent. He also claimed the university had become a "social justice factory" where intellectual exploration is no longer possible and the focus is on race, gender, victimhood.[2] Perhaps the most telling comment in Boghossian's letter of resignation was: "Students at Portland State are not being taught to think. Rather, they are being trained to mimic the moral certainty of ideologues. Faculty and administrators have abdicated the university's truth-seeking mission and instead drive intolerance of divergent beliefs and opinions."[3]

Professor Boghossian's letter of resignation summed up succinctly and well what is happening in American colleges and universities nationwide. "Wokeness" has become the norm not the exception. Professors who still believe in the stated purposes of higher education are punished, discriminated against, and harassed. Students who want an education instead of a high-priced Leftist indoctrination are attacked and vilified. What Professor Boghossian described at

Portland State University could be said about most colleges and universities in the United States.

AMERICAN CULTURE: THEN AND NOW

Sociocultural changes occur so gradually many fail to realize they are even happening. This is the phenomenon known as *boiling-the-frog*, a favorite strategy of the Left. But then-versus-now comparisons demonstrate just how much American culture has changed over the years. Public schools used to operate hand-in-hand with parents and families. The values taught at home were reinforced at school. Teachers did not think they had the right to overrule or undermine parents. Students were responsible for their schoolwork and behavior and were held accountable for both. In disagreements between teachers and students, parents invariably sided with teachers. Teachers had the backing of the school, parents, and the community.

We attended public elementary schools for grades one through six and cannot remember a school day not beginning with a Bible reading, the Lord's Prayer, and the Pledge of Allegiance. Christianity was the norm. We can remember being called on the carpet by public school teachers for skipping Sunday school or church. Denying our truancy did no good because they knew we weren't in attendance because they were. In high school, we played football. Before taking the field for Friday night games, we knelt in the locker room and listened in reverent silence as our coach prayed for us. Then, before the opening kickoff a local minister would pray over the stadium's public address system. All the spectators in the stands stood and bowed their heads. Today you would have to look hard to find a public school willing to stand up to the ACLU and allow, much less require, Bible reading and prayer before class.

Neighborhoods were much different when we were growing up. We did not lock our doors, other parents in the neighborhood felt comfortable correcting our bad behavior, and we could play outside unsupervised all day with no fear of pedophiles, drug pushers, or child molesters. In fact, during the summer months our parents expected us to "go outside and play" after breakfast and not return until lunch. The routine was repeated after lunch. We could range far and wide in our neighborhood with no thought of danger, all the while knowing if we stepped out of line an adult would be on the telephone to our parents within minutes.

Today adults are actually afraid to confront miscreant young people. If they are not attacked by the caitiff, they will probably be sued by their helicopter parents. Not only do families lock their doors these days, many have installed expensive security systems, and with good reason. Home invasions and break-ins have become common crimes in most communities, especially upper-middle class and wealthy neighborhoods where predatory youth use burglary to finance their drug habits. Telling your children to go out and play and be back by supper is unheard of these days. Kidnapping and human trafficking have robbed today's youngsters of this freedom.

Rick Scarborough posed a pertinent question about the past versus the current state of affairs in America: "How could we go from a society where divorce was almost non-existent, the church was the center of the community, the school's greatest discipline problems were talking and chewing gum, and neighborhoods seldom witnessed 'for sale' signs to a society where divorce has become the rule, church is considered irrelevant, schools are installing metal detectors, and the average family moves twelve times in only forty years?"[4] The answer to Scarborough's question is found in the creeping secularization of American society. As a country, we have turned from the religion of God to the religion of secular humanism. We have given up biblical values and embraced moral relativism.

LEFTIST ORTHODOXY PERMEATES THE CULTURE

As was just shown in the previous section, the radical Left has made "progress" in the culture war it is waging against God, country, and Conservatives. The American family has been shattered, our public schools have been turned into Leftist indoctrination centers, and the church is reeling from the effects of feel-good theology. Then there is the sordid state of affairs in the entertainment industry, one of the Left's most effective weapons. Having won these victories in the battle for America's soul, the radical Left is now focused on one of its most cherished prizes: higher education.

The Left knows if it can control the faculties, administrations, and curriculums of our nation's institutions of higher education, it can control the minds of each successive generation of America's leaders. Christians and Conservatives cannot allow this to happen. Every victory of the Left mentioned throughout this book has been aided by Christians and Conservatives who chose to retreat rather than stand and fight. We cannot afford to retreat any longer. It is time to fight back. Making Americans aware of the critical need to take a stand and equipping them to fight back is the purpose of this book.

Marxist socialism has failed everywhere it has been tried including the Soviet Union, North Korea, Vietnam, Cuba, Venezuela, and China. China has become an economic powerhouse, not because of Marxist socialism but because the communist government finally admitted its failings and established capitalist enterprise zones throughout the country. Those who are advancing a Marxist socialist agenda are fools because they not only deny the existence and sovereignty of God, they persist in trying to impose a blatantly failed system everywhere it has been tried.

This book is not just for college students and their parents. It is for all Americans who are concerned about the

Leftist tidal wave that has swept over our country covering
society in the detritus of moral decay. If you are concerned
about America's future and want to take a stand, the college
or university campus is a good place to start. It is here your
efforts have the most potential to bear fruit. The Left understands this and is acting accordingly. Consequently, it is
critical that Christians and Conservatives take up the cause
and fight back.

AUTHORS' BIOGRAPHIES

Oliver L. North is a combat-decorated U.S. Marine, #1 best-selling author, founder of small businesses, and holder of three U.S. patents. For seventeen years he was a syndicated columnist and host of *War Stories* on FOX News Channel. In May 2018, he retired from FOX News to serve as the 66th president of the National Rifle Association of America.

North was born in San Antonio, Texas, in 1943, graduated from the U.S. Naval Academy in 1968, and served twenty-two years as a U.S. Marine. His awards for service in combat include the Silver Star, the Bronze Star for valor, and two Purple Hearts for wounds in action.

From 1983–86 he served as Counter-Terrorism Coordinator on the National Security Council staff. He helped plan the rescue of U.S. students on Grenada, the liberation of American hostages, the capture of the *Achille Lauro* hijackers, and the raids on Muammar Gadhafi's terror bases—after which he was targeted for assassination by Abu Nidal's Islamic Jihad. President Ronald Reagan described him as "an American hero."

North has authored more than twenty best-selling books and is cofounder of Freedom Alliance, an organization serving wounded U.S. military personnel and their families. He is widely acclaimed for award-winning FOX News coverage of more than sixty U.S. units in combat and his Freedom Alliance "Hero College Scholarships" for children of service members killed or permanently disabled in the line of duty. He currently hosts a highly popular podcast on his YouTube channel, *Real American Heroes*. Yet, he says his greatest achievement is being "the God-fearing husband of one, father of four, and grandfather of eighteen."

LtCol North and his wife, Betsy, live in Virginia. In November 2018, they celebrated their 50th anniversary. He is currently founder and CEO of Fidelis Publishing and Fidelis Media.

His newest book, *The Giant Awakes*, is now available at olivernorth.com, faithfultext.com, and all book retailers.

Dr. David L. Goetsch served in higher education for forty-three years holding the positions of instructor, professor, department chair, division director, dean, provost, and vice-president. He holds an associate degree, bachelor's degree, four master's degrees, and a doctorate degree and has taught in the fields of business and political science.

During his career Dr. Goetsch was selected as Professor of the Year five times, Florida's Technical/Business Educator of the Year in 1986, Master Teacher by the National Institute for Staff and Program Development in 1990, and Master Teacher by Phi Delta Kappa in 1990. In 1984, Dr. Goetsch's program at Northwest Florida State College was chosen as the Outstanding Program in America (Region 10) by the U.S. Secretary of Education.

Dr. Goetsch is a Marine Corps veteran and a member of the Florida Veterans' Hall of Fame (Class of 2016). He is the author of seventy-eight books, several of which are best-sellers that have been translated into various foreign languages.

Dr. Archie Jones is a teacher, librarian, and professor who has taught various subjects at the college and high school levels, including political science, American history, literature, and writing. He is the author of eight books on Christianity in early American society, America's early state constitutions, the Articles of Confederation, and the U.S.

Constitution. Dr. Jones is the author of *The Gateway to Liberty: The Constitutional Power of the Tenth Amendment.* His dissertation, "Christianity in the Constitution: The Intended Meaning of the Religion Clauses of the First Amendment and the Intended Role of Religion in American Life," is devoted to recovering the truth about the First Amendment.

NOTES

CHAPTER 1

1. Hillsdale College, Larry Arnn speech adapted for *Imprimis* 51, no. 11 (November 2022), https://imprimis.hillsdale.edu/education-as-a-battleground/.

CHAPTER 3

1. "Declaration of Independence: A Transcription," National Archives, https://www.archives.gov/founding-docs/declaration-transcript, accessed December 30, 2022.
2. "Mayflower and Mayflower Compact," plimoth.org/for-students/homework-help/mayflower-and-mayflower-compact, accessed September 8, 2021.
3. "Articles of Confederation (1777)," National Archives, https://www.archives.gov/milestone-documents/articles-of-confederation, accessed September 8, 2021.
4. Jun-Youb, Lee, "A History of God at Harvard," *The Harvard Crimson*, January 28, 2020, https://www.thecrimson.com/article/2020/1/28/lee-history-god-harvard/.
5. Lee, "A History of God at Harvard."
6. Patrick Henry, "Give Me Liberty or Give Me Death!," https://www.colonialwilliamsburg.org/learn/deep-dives/give-me-liberty-or-give-me-death/, accessed September 8, 2021.
7. Henry, "Give Me Liberty or Give Me Death!"

8. Benjamin Franklin (quoting Psalm 127:1), Speech to the Constitutional Convention, https://www.americanrhetoric.com/speeches/benfranklin.htm, accessed August 13, 2021.

9. Thomas Jefferson, *Notes on the State of Virginia*, Query 18 (1781–1785), https://teachingamericanhistory.org/document/notes-on-the-state-of-virginia-2/, accessed August 13, 2021.

10. George Washington's Mount Vernon "Thanksgiving Proclamation of 1789," https://www.mountvernon.org/education/primary-source-collections/primary-source-collections/article/thanksgiving-proclamation-of-1789/, accessed August 13, 2021.

11. "From John Adams to Massachusetts Militia, 11 October 1798," Founders Online, https://founders.archives.gov/documents/Adams/99-02-02-3102, accessed August 13, 2021.

12. "James Monroe Second Annual Message," The American Presidency Project, https://www.presidency.ucsb.edu/documents/second-annual-message-1, accessed August 13, 2021.

13. Justia U.S. Supreme Court Center. "Church of the Holy Trinity v. United States, 143 U.S. 457 (1892)," Retrieved from https://supreme.justia.com/cases/federal/US/143/457/ on August 13, 2021.

14. John Jay, October 12, 1816, in *The Correspondence and Public Papers of John Jay*, ed. Henry P. Johnston (New York: G. P. Putnam & Sons, 1893; repr. New York: Burt Franklin, 1970), Vol. IV, 393.

15. John Jay in *The Founders on Religion: A Book of Quotations*, ed. James H. Hutson (Princeton, NJ: Princeton Univ. Press, 2005), 52.

16. James Wilson, *The Works of the Honourable James Wilson* (Philadelphia: Bronson and Chauncey, 1804), 67.

17. Justia U.S. Supreme Court Center. "Vidal v. Girard's Executors, 43 U.S. 127 (1844)," https://supreme.justia.com/cases/federal/us/43/127/, accessed August 13, 2021.

18. Reclaiming America for Christ, "The House of Representatives Rules We Are a Christian Nation," www.reclaimamericaforchrist.org/2010/11/24/the-house-of-representatives-rules-we-are-a-christian-nation/, accessed August 13, 2021.

19. "Reclaiming America for Christ."

20. "Constitution of Massachusetts (1780)," www.nhinet.org/ccs/docs/ma-1780.htm, accessed August 16, 2021.

21. Constitution of South Carolina (1778), "South Carolina Constitution Conservation," https://scarchivesand historyfoundation.org/south-carolina-constitution-conservation/, accessed August 16, 2021.

CHAPTER 4

1. Charlie Sykes, "The Dumbing Down of College Curriculums," The Daily Signal, August 29, 2016, https://www.dailysignal.com/2016/08/29/the-dumbing-down-of-college-curriculums/.

2. Sykes, "The Dumbing Down of College Curriculums."

3. Sykes.

4. Sykes.

5. Matthew Lynch, "How Dumb Downed Education Is Creating a National Security Crisis," The Edvocate, August 20, 2019, https://www.theedadvocate.org/how-dumbed-down-education-is-creating-a-national-security-crisis/.

6. Arthur Herman, "America's High-Tech STEM Crisis," Forbes, September 10, 2018,

7. https://www.forbes.com/sites/arthurherman/2018/09/10/americas-high-tech-stem-crisis/?sh=4722c113f0a2.

8. Herman, "America's High-Tech STEM Crisis."

CHAPTER 5

1. Jordan B. Peterson, "Trouble at the University of Amsterdam," Jordan B. Peterson blog, October 31, 2018, https://www.jordanbpeterson.com/political-correctness/trouble-at-the-university-of-amsterdam/.
2. Bureau of Labor Statistics, U.S. Department of Labor, "The Economics Daily," August 30, 2016, https://www.bls.gov/opub/ted/2016/college-tuition-and-fees-increase-63-percent-since-january-2006.htm.
3. Melanie Hanson, "Average Cost of College & Tuition," Education Data, updated October 24, 2022, https://educationdata.org/average-cost-of-college#.
4. Hanson, "Average Cost of College & Tuition."

CHAPTER 6

1. "Humanist Manifesto II," American Humanist Association, https://americanhumanist.org/what-is-humanism/manifesto2/, accessed August 28, 2021.
2. Website of the American Humanist Association, https://americanhumanist.org, accessed August 28, 2021.
3. John Dunphy, "A Religion for a New Age," *The Humanist* 43, January/February 1983, https://johnjdunphy.medium.com/a-religion-for-a-new-age-f812839c4cb8.
4. "Humanism and Its Aspirations: Human Manifesto III, a Successor to the Humanist Manifesto of 1933," https://americanhumanist.org/what-is-humanism/manifesto3/, accessed August 28, 2021.
5. Perry L. Glanzer and Todd C. Ream, "Educating Different Types of Citizens: Identity, Tradition, Moral Education," *Journal of College and Character* 9, no. 4 (April 2008): 1, https://www.tandfonline.com/doi/epdf/10.2202/1940-1639.1141.

6. Anne Colby, "Whose Values Anyway?" *Journal of College and Character* 3, no. 5 (2002), https://www.tandfonline.com/doi/epdf/10.2202/1940-1639.1322.

7. Ryan Dobson, *Be Intolerant: Because Some Things Are Just Stupid* (Carol Stream, IL: Tyndale House, 2003), 55.

8. Dobson, *Be Intolerant*, 55–56.

9. Dobson, 49.

10. Dobson, 50–55.

11. Emma Goldberg, "The New Chief Chaplain at Harvard? An Atheist," *New York Times*, August 26, 2021, https://www.nytimes.com/2021/08/26/us/harvard-chaplain-greg-epstein.html.

CHAPTER 7

1. Phyllis Schafly, "Diversity Dishonesty on College Campuses," The Phyllis Schafly Report, Vol. 35, No. 9 (April 2002), https://eagleforum.org/psr/2002/apr02/psrapr02.shtml.

2. David Horowitz, "The Surreal World of the Progressive Left," FrontPage, January 25, 2008.

3. "Defending Religious Freedom," Alliance Defense Fund (name changed to Alliance Defending Freedom in 2012), http://www.alliancedefensefund.org/issues/religious/freedom/default.aspx?cid=2573, accessed August 31, 2021.

4. Ben Shapiro, *Brainwashed: How Universities Indoctrinate America's Youth* (Nashville: Thomas Nelson, 2004), 85.

5. Shapiro, *Brainwashed*.

6. John Indo in Letters to the Editor, "Logic for Fundamentalists?" *Free Inquiry*, Vol. 2, No. 1, (Winter 1981), 3, https://cdn.centerforinquiry.org/wp-content/uploads/sites/26/1981/01/22161304/p03.pdf.

7. David L. Goetsch and Archie P. Jones, *Liberal Tyranny in Higher Education* (Powder Springs, GA: American Vision Press, 2009), 74–77.
8. Patrick J. Buchanan, *The Death of the West* (New York: Thomas Dunne Books, an imprint of St. Martin's Press, 2002), 173.
9. Jerry Bergman, *Slaughter of the Dissidents* (Southworth, WA: Leafcutter Press, 2008), 165.
10. Bergman, *Slaughter of the Dissidents*, 161–63.
11. Bergman, 166.
12. Bergman, 164.
13. "Dr. Guillermo Gonzalez and Academic Persecution," Discovery Institute, February 8, 2008, http://www.discovery.org/a/2939/.
14. "Dr. Guillermo Gonzalez and Academic Persecution."
15. "Biography of Dr. Guillermo Gonzalez," Discovery Institute, May 16, 2007, https://www.discovery.org/a/4058/.
16. "Intelligent Design Was the Issue After All (Updated)," Discovery Institute, https://www.discovery.org/m/securepdfs/2021/02/ID_was_the_Issue_Gonzalez_Tenure.pdf, accessed September 7, 2021.
17. "Intelligent Design Was the Issue After All (Updated)."
18. "Intelligent Design Was the Issue After All (Updated)."

CHAPTER 8

1. Transcription of *The Joe Rogan Experience* podcast, episode 1070 featuring Jordan B. Peterson, February 27, 2018, https://erikamentari.wordpress.com/2018/02/27/jre-1070-jordan-peterson-transcript/.
2. "Lopez v. John Matteson, in his individual and official capacities as Professor of Speech at Los Angeles City College, Defendant," FindLaw, https://caselaw.findlaw.com/us-9th-circuit/1538732.html, accessed December 29, 2022.

3. Daniel A. Feldman, *Critical Thinking: Make Strategic Decisions with Confidence* (Menlo Park, CA: Crisp Publications, 2002), 7.

4. Feldman, *Critical Thinking*, 62–68.

5. Voddie Baucham Jr., *The Ever-Loving Truth: Can Faith Thrive in a Post-Christian Culture?* (Nashville: Broadman & Holman, 2006), 88.

6. Bay Buchanan, "The Art of Debate," in *The Conservative Guide to Campus Activism* by Patrick X. Cayle and Ron Robinson (Herndon, VA: Young America's Foundation, 2005), 10–13.

EPILOGUE

1. Rick Scarborough, *Enough Is Enough: A Practical Guide to Political Action* (Lake Mary, FL: Front Line, 2004), 6.

2. Sam Dorman, "Portland State Professor Resigns," FOX News, September 8, 2021, https://www.foxnews.com/us/portland-professor-resigns-boghossian.

3. Dorman, "Portland State Professor Resigns."

4. Scarborough, *Enough Is Enough*, 7.